Moms' Lifesavers

Tips to Make Life Easier For New Mothers

CHRISTINE COHEN, M.Ed. & JOANNE TOCCI, O.T.

Laurel Canyon Publishing

Published in the United States of America by Laurel Canyon Publishing

Library of Congress Control Number: 2006929416

ISBN-13   978-0-9786530-0-2
ISBN-10   0-9786530-0-9

Design by Lynn Wood Design
Cover Illustration by Joanne Andrews

Printed in the United States of America
First Edition

To order additional copies of this book check us out on the web at **www.momslifesavers.com**
or write:
Mother Hen Books
14805 Lake Terrace
Rockville, MD 20853

Dedication

For Scott, Minna and Kaia – the loves of my life.
For my wonderful parents, Gunter and Renate Kostka.
C.C.

For VJ, Tino, Lucas, Jessica, and Sara, the people
who have given me the privileged name of "mother".
And, to my mother – a true super-mom!
J.T.

Table of Contents

Introduction

Mothers everywhere lead extremely hectic lives! Whether it's balancing a career while raising children or managing a household as a stay-at-home mom. Throw in schedules, to-do lists, and other activities, and time and energy are stretched thin. As mothers, we realized the need for a quick and easy reference guide with common issues regarding babies and young children.

We feel very blessed to have a wonderful group of friends and family to share our experiences with. Reveling in the tribulations and commiserating in the trials of raising a young child, we had many invaluable brainstorming opportunities to assist us over the first-time mother hurdles. Now that we are the proud mothers of six children between us, we want to share these tips with others, whom we hope may benefit from the myriad of advice we've gathered.

Knowing that all mothers have creative ideas of their own, we surveyed over one hundred women from around the country, obtaining "tried and true" tips and suggestions on a wide range of parenting topics. And did we assemble a treasure trove of ideas and thoughtful responses. The end result is a book that provides a wealth of practical, helpful advice and information…without a lot of time spent reading! It is presented in a quick-reference format for ease of gathering suggestions on how to handle various infant, toddler, and preschool situations.

Each section has space allotted for writing down your own ideas, advice, and information found in other parenting materials. This allows for the continued compilation of ideas, perhaps to share with someone about to have a baby, or even to pass on to the next generation.

Our advanced professional training in Special Education and Occupational Therapy has given us a comprehensive background in child development and education. The section "Development from Birth to Age Five" was provided to steer you down the developmental path, with space for recording dates and special reflections when your child reaches milestones along the way.

Take good care of yourself as you give endlessly to your children on this amazing journey. Think of the book as one huge play date with a handful of other moms in the same room, offering heartfelt remedies to common issues surrounding parenthood. We hope you will benefit from these "pearls of wisdom", and that they help you to find some solace amidst these busy and joyful times.

Enjoy!

Christine Cohen and Joanne Tocci

I. WELCOME BABY

Preparing for the Little Arrival

You're having your first child, the "nesting" instinct hits, and you head out to stock up on baby supplies. Standing in a baby store, you find yourself faced with HUNDREDS of childcare products, along with a kindly salesperson trying to sell you all of them! This can indeed be an overwhelming experience. Here's a must-have, bare bones list of necessities to have on hand when the baby comes home. Compiled by moms who have been there, this should help to streamline your shopping expedition.

FOR BABY

Clothing

- Lots of onesies and sleepers to cut down on laundry.
- Hats and socks.
- Gowns are great for quick and easy diaper changes.
- Sleep sack (a wearable blanket that zippers on and off).
- Easy wash and wear cotton outfits with snaps ("fancy" clothing is cute, but not as comfortable for baby).

Diaper Changing

- Disposable diapers.
- Changing table pad and washable covers.
- Disposable wipes.
- Diaper cream (Desitin, Aquaphor, or A+D ointment).
- Vaseline, baby oil.
- For circumcision care, use Bacitracin or Vaseline in a tube, and gauze.
- Diaper pail, such as the "Diaper Genie" or one that doesn't require refills (which get expensive), such as the "Diaper Champ"; stick-up deodorizer to put inside the pail.
- Basket of changing supplies to keep in a different part of the house where you and baby spend a lot of time.
- Something fun for dads: Daddy Diaper Duty Emergency Tool Kit has all necessary equipment for the dads! (www.daddyshop.com)

Bathing

- Johnson 'n Johnson disposable baby wash cloths.
- Soap-free, hypoallergenic baby wash and lotion.
- Tiny wash cloths.
- Sponge mat to lay baby on to bathe, or comfortable tub (lay a towel inside of it first to make it softer).
- Hooded towels.
- Baby powder with corn starch.

Baby Care

- Infant nail clippers.
- Thermometer.
- For umbilical cord care use rubbing alcohol and cotton balls.
- Aspirator bulb and saline drops to moisten and clean the nasal passages.
- Johnson 'n Johnson's "Baby Relief Kit" – briefcase style kit with products for fever, diaper rash, upset stomachs, coughs and colds.

Feeding

- Burping cloths.
- Lots of bibs.
- If nursing, refer to breastfeeding section. Prepare a "back-up" plan in case nursing doesn't work out.
- If you're bottle feeding, a CASE of formula so you don't have to worry about running out (you can order online directly from the companies, and they don't usually charge for shipping).
- Bottles – at least six, cleaned and ready to go (disposable bottles require liners that you have to continuously buy, which can get expensive over time, however many mother's enjoy the convenience of them.)
- Choose a bottle that you're sure to stick with, as babies often won't switch nipples once you start on a certain type.
- Electric baby bottle warmer.

Nighttime

- Crib or co-sleeper beside your bed so baby is nearby.
- Waterproof mattress pad.
- Crib bumper.
- Bedding for crib – the zip on and off sheets work nicely.
- Nightlight for feedings and diaper changes and a light with dimmer switch or 3-way touch lamp.

Extras

- Hypoallergenic baby detergent for washing clothes, at least initially.
- A pacifier, just in case you need it (save the one from the hospital!).
- Thin, stretchy blankets for swaddling. You can also buy easy-to-use, pre-shaped swaddling blankets.
- Flannel receiving blankets or cloth diapers, for swaddling, burping, and a million other uses!
- A few Lamaze infant toys.
- For the colder months, a "cozy cover" for the car seat.
- Cool-mist humidifier.

FOR MOM

Care for You

- Grandma, so you can get some sleep!
- Items for your recovery: Maxipads, Preparation H, Tucks Pads with witch hazel, Mederma scar cream for C-sections, Tylenol or Motrin, squirt bottle for gentle cleansing and diluting urine.
- A nice, soothing CD for relaxing baby and mom.
- Something special for you to pamper yourself with (try www.pajamagram.com).
- Love, patience, support from family and friends.

More Lifesavers

Feeding Baby

- A very comfortable chair to sit in (glider or a rocking chair) and foot stool for support.
- Side table to hold drinks and nursing supplies.
- Nursing pillow, such as a Boppy.
- Nursing pads (cotton, wool, or disposable) to protect clothing from leaks. Contoured pads have a more comfortable fit.
- Two or more nursing bras (as they need to be washed frequently) and pajamas.
- Pump for nursing moms.
- Breastfeeding reading materials for help, along with phone numbers of people who can assist you.

Feeding Yourself and Family

- Lots of previously made dinners in your freezer.
- Phone numbers and menus of local restaurants that deliver.
- Healthy snack foods that are easy to grab, such as muffins, string cheese, grapes or crackers.
- Accept offers of help from family and friends to prepare a meal every other day for week two – that's when your meals run out, baby gets needier, and you are tired!

Plaster molds of bulging tummy. You can do it yourself!

YOU NEED:

2 rolls Plaster of Paris gauze strips

Scissors

1 bucket filled halfway with warm water

Vaseline

Trash bag

Plastic shower curtain

A helper

WHAT TO DO:

- Cut 2 foot strips of the gauze strips, enough for three layers on your belly.
- Cover entire belly area with Vaseline (very important to keep yourself protected and for ease upon removal).
- With a friend helping, soak each strip in warm water.
- Stand on the shower curtain to protect the floor.
- Start to place wet strips on belly and make one even overlapping layer (horizontal layers work best).
- Continue to place two additional layers on the first layer (you will feel the plaster hardening quickly and get heavy).
- Leave the mold on your belly to dry for about 10-15 minutes.
- Remove mold and place on trash bag to dry overnight.
- You can have a "goddess moment" and paint it yourself… or wait until your child is old enough to help with the design themselves!

Extras

- Good supervision and maintenance of routines for other siblings.
- Help with chores such as cleaning and laundry; enlist a mother's helper or teenage babysitter.
- Thank-you notes and stamps in the house ready to go.

Equipment

- Car seat you can carry in and out of the car and attach to stroller.
- Changing table set at proper height so you won't strain your back.
- Bassinet.
- Baby monitor – the two-way ones are nice so you can communicate with a spouse if need be, and when the child gets older you can talk back to them.
- Bouncy seat – great for baby to lie in or sleep in. Seats with vibrators and music are great.
- Portable swing.
- Camera – digital, regular, or handycam camcorder for instant DVD's.
- Portable phone – hands free capability is helpful.
- Good baby health book – see Parent Book Section.

PRENATAL IDEAS FOR MOM

- Take a pre-natal or Lamaze class – it's worth every minute for good birth training.
- Register with www.babycenter.com for day to day information about your developing baby and tummy.
- Pre-natal yoga, water aerobics, and massage.
- Fetal imaging.
- First Aid and CPR class.

FINDING A PEDIATRICIAN

The decision of whom to entrust with the healthcare of your child is an important one to make. Start by finding out if your insurance provider has a list of pre-approved, board certified doctors you must choose from. Also, ask friends and family for the names of doctors they are familiar with and trust, as personal references are extremely helpful. Schedule appointments to interview several potential doctors prior to your delivery date.

Good Questions to Consider

- Does the physician share your philosophies with regard to topics such as immunization schedules, breastfeeding, and developmental milestones?
- Do you feel a good rapport with the doctor? Are they friendly? Would you feel comfortable asking any and all questions you may have without fearing judgment?
- What are the office hours? Do they offer evening appointments?
- Do they offer walk-in sick calls? Everyday? Weekends?
- Do they accept and bill your insurance?
- Is there a separate waiting room for sick vs. well children?
- Is there someone available to answer questions at any time over the phone?
- What is the "on-call" policy?
- Will your child always see the same pediatrician, or will they see different ones in the practice? Will they see nurse practitioners?
- Will there be sufficient appointment time allotted for asking questions?

Advice From the Trenches: Part One

Most of us have said at one time or another, "If only I had known THAT earlier…" Well, here is your opportunity to soak up some "pearls of wisdom" from moms – both young and old – who have been where you are now!

BEFORE THE BIRTH

- One month before your baby is due, have your hospital bag packed and ready to go. Make sure you have all baby supplies and clothes organized and prepared for your arrival home. You never know when you'll go into labor!

- Borrow, borrow, and borrow! Ask for hand-me-downs for as much as you can (except for crib and car seats).

- Don't over-decorate a nursery in a baby theme… you will be bored with it and they will outgrow it quickly.

- Don't spend a lot of money on expensive nursery furniture and accessories. Save your money for other expenses.

- Prior to baby's birth you'll probably receive quite a few things as gifts, so stick with the basics.

- One month before the birth of sub-sequent babies, have older children's bags packed and ready to go, if needed. Include any lists or instructions you want your babysitter to have. Prepare a plan for who is going to look after your children, depending on whether it's the middle of the night or a weekday.

AFTER THE BIRTH

- Never hesitate to contact your pediatrician with ANY questions you have about your newborn. A good office will have no problem answering questions over the phone.

- Ask for and accept help as needed, and screen advice – no one knows your baby better than you!

- Do whatever it takes to have a shower and get dressed everyday. Even if you have to get up earlier, you'll feel much better. Lounging around in PJ's all day without a shower is very unmotivating! Buy a few nice pieces of clothing you can wear, even if they're in a bigger size than you hope you'll be wearing 6 months from now, so you'll feel better about yourself.

- Upon a new baby's arrival, don't feel guilty about allowing your older children to watch more TV or movies than you normally would for the first few weeks. Your baby needs your attention, and you need your rest!

- If you don't have a dishwasher, use paper plates and cups for the first couple of weeks for convenience.

Take the phone off the hook and sleep when the baby sleeps.

- Don't keep a "quiet" house when baby is sleeping. Try to have some background noise (radio, TV) so that baby doesn't get used to and dependent upon silence for sleeping.

- If nursing, consider using a co-sleeper or bassinet and nurse your newborn in bed with you until they can sleep for 5 or 6 hours without feeding so you'll get more sleep.

- Pump right from the beginning so that your husband and family can assist in feeding; this will give you a break and help to ensure that the baby will take to a bottle.

- If you have a baby boy who was circumcised, put Vaseline directly on the front of the diaper so his penis doesn't stick to it.
- Cut baby's fingernails and toenails while they're sleeping – it's much easier!
- Find a way to get outside with baby at least once a day, even in cold weather.
- Don't sanitize yourself or your house too much – your baby's immune system will be healthier when exposed to SOME germs.
- If you're interested in sign language but don't want to teach the whole language, then at 7 months start using signs for a few select words, such as "drink," "more," "all done," and "eat." By 9 months they should start using the signs independently which will make feeding time easier.

POST-PARTUM DEPRESSION

It is not uncommon to suffer the "baby blues" following the birth of your baby. During the first one to two weeks you may find yourself tearful, having mood swings, being irritable, and having difficulty sleeping. This can be due to the sudden change in hormone levels, or an anti-climactic feeling after the birth of the baby.

Unlike these "blues," post-partum depression is longer-lasting and more serious, affecting 10-15% of women. You may experience deep feelings of hope-lessness and despair, feel panicky, lethargic, have obsessive thoughts, or lack self-esteem and concentration. Should you notice these early warning signals it is critical to seek medical attention for this disorder, as with early treatment it can usually resolve within a few weeks. Don't suffer when there is help available.

More Lifesavers

Doula: The Woman Caregiver

A doula is someone who provides non-clinical support before, during, and following the birthing process. After developing a personal relationship with you, a doula helps to achieve your ideal birth. For some, this includes pain coping measures for a natural birth, or various coping strategies prior to some form of pain medication. Experienced doulas will have the knowledge to discern what is normal in the course of the average term pregnancy and labor, and will be able to discuss options with you. They will help you work through different birth scenarios and provide non-biased, research-based information regarding statistics and birth outcomes. For example, if you are considering moving into a different position – how might that affect the baby or your labor? What positions are least likely to stress your body and the baby, while being the most effective at progressing your labor?

The doula provides constant support twenty-four hours a day, including the time spent at home in early labor. In addition to providing physical support, such as massage and relaxation techniques, a large part of what a doula helps with is mom's emotional state. Most women will come to a point in labor where they are tired and feel like they can't continue. Your doula is there to listen and buoy you up when you need a lift!

Ideally, the doula will continue seeing the mother postpartum, both at the hospital and at home. Even if a woman did not have a doula for her birth, postpartum doulas are available and can be a huge help to mom. Paid hourly, they can be an extra pair of hands – rocking/holding the baby so mom can rest or bathe, cooking meals, light housework, or grocery shopping. They may be able to assist with breastfeeding if they have additional certifications in that specialty.

There have been many research studies showing that delivering with a doula decreases anxiety, shortens labor, improves birth outcome and increases maternal – infant bonding. By removing fear, women are able to embrace the experience and recall their birth happily, because they were completely supported and made well informed choices along the way.

Kimberly Putney, Doula

Breastfeeding

One of the most important decisions you will make is whether or not to breastfeed your baby. Choosing to do so is often the most challenging aspect of newborn care. It is, without doubt, an art that requires education, assistance, practice, and patience!

Despite the challenges, there are numerous benefits in choosing to nurse your baby. It is economical, as you don't have to buy expensive formula. Breast milk is always ready to go at the right temperature with no extra equipment required. It is the perfect food – easily digestible, packed with vitamins and minerals, boosts baby's immune system, helps to prevent allergies, and offers protection from infection. Beneficial substances such as DHA (fatty acid that promotes eye and brain development) are provided through breast milk.

The benefits of nursing extend to mother as well. It helps the uterus return to its pre-pregnancy size, and burning about 500 calories per day it can help women lose extra baby weight. Research has shown that breastfeeding can reduce the risk of breast, uterine and ovarian cancers, and decreases the incidence of osteoporosis.

Some disadvantages for mothers are that it takes a lot of hard work and is time consuming. You are tied down to feeding schedules, and if you are not pumping others cannot help feed the baby. This may leave other family members feel left-out in the process. Dietary restrictions for mothers may be necessary to avoid foods that cause babies to have upset stomachs and fussiness.

Whatever decision you make, be confident that is the right decision for you and your baby! If you do decide to breastfeed, then the following tips will be helpful in ensuring success.

GETTING HELP

- Buy and read a good nursing book ahead of time, to help with problem-solving as needed.
- Consult a lactation expert at the hospital and schedule a home visit before you leave to make sure you're doing things right.
- Have a friend who's nursed successfully visit and help. Plan to have her come on day two or three when your milk comes in.
- Be aware that if you have had a C-section, especially one which was planned, your milk's arrival may be delayed due to the trauma of surgery.
- Don't suffer with any pain or problems – phone a lactation consultant, La Leche League, or experienced friend and ask for assistance.

IN THE BEGINNING

- Purchase nursing bras that you can undo and fasten with one hand, which is especially helpful when you're nursing around other people. Try it before you buy it.
- For the first six weeks – nurse 'em, nurse 'em, nurse 'em. Forget about schedules early on – it's normal if they nurse ALL the time – kick back and relax!
- It takes a while to work out all the kinks, at least two to three weeks so try not to quit too early! Having the determination that this is the best option for you and your baby will get you through the rough times.
- At latch-on clench teeth and count to ten slowly, to help get through the initial discomfort.
- Use a pillow or "Boppy" for good positioning of the baby and less stress on your back.
- At the first sign of engorgement use hot compresses and steamy hot showers, and KEEP NURSING.

- It can be painful, but it hurts less and less as time goes on and gets easier after your nipples toughen and your milk supply regulates.
- Listen to soothing music will help you and your baby to relax – they WILL pick up on your tension, and may not nurse as well.

GENERAL ADVICE

- Maximum nursing time for both sides should be 30 minutes – 15 minutes per side. If baby is nursing longer than this they are not getting any more milk, and are sucking for comfort only and exhausting you unnecessarily.
- Try to get baby to fully empty one breast before moving on to the next one, in order to receive both the foremilk which contains more sugar and water and the hindmilk which is higher in fat and calories.
- Warm compresses and hot showers before feedings work well to help increase comfort and flow of milk. Cold compresses work well in between feedings to help decrease swelling due to engorgement.
- If your baby is too sleepy to drink a full feeding, try undressing them, changing diaper, rubbing feet and back of baby while nursing, stroking with a damp cloth, and switching nursing sides frequently.
- If baby can't keep up with milk flow and gags after latching on, latch baby on to achieve let-down, take baby off as soon as milk is flowing and catch milk with cloth diaper (letting it squirt into diaper for a second), then latch baby back on once milk slows down.
- If you have a plugged duct, lie baby on their back on your bed or floor and position yourself over top of baby so that when baby sucks, their chin is over the plugged duct; follow with hot shower while massaging or manually pumping sore spots; follow by rest; repeat sequence making sure you feed on sore side first.

- If you suffer from prolonged pain, fever, or contained, painful, red areas or streaks on the breast, you may have a breast infection (mastitis). Consult your health-care provider immediately, as medication may be needed.
- Slings are great for carrying baby, especially when you want to discreetly nurse in public, as baby is positioned and ready to go.

Next to birthing, this may be the most difficult, yet rewarding, act of child-bearing. It takes a while to get used to the routine of feedings, to gain a comfort in the amount of milk you are producing, and to feel connected, but not shackled to your new baby. Relax! Try not to feed the baby in a rush within the first couple of months – you will increase the odds that breastfeeding will be rewarding for both of you!

HELP FOR SORE NIPPLES

- Seek initial assistance at the hospital from the lactation consultant to ensure a proper latch-on. At home, call a lactation consultant or another mom for assistance and advice if you have problems.
- Try various nursing positions to get baby to latch on different areas of the areola (pink circle around nipple), in order to distribute pressures differently each time such as football hold, cradle hold, crossover hold, lying down (side-lying and reclining).
- Even if you have a sore area on your nipple, continue to nurse from that side.
- Place expressed milk on nipples and allow to air dry after feedings.
- Try using cooling gel pads (Soothies) that fit inside your bra.
- Use cold packs (even a bag of frozen veggies!) before feeding to numb sore nipples.

- Pump or use manual extraction to give nipples a rest.
- Put lanolin cream (Lansinoh) on before you begin nursing, and right after (be sure to use nursing pads as it can stain your clothing).
- If your milk comes in and you are engorged, or you are starting a feeding with engorged breasts, pump for a couple of minutes just before feeding in order to "deflate" the breast a bit (picture a balloon!) this will help with attaining a proper latch-on, and also helps with building up a milk supply for you.
- Breastshells are plastic "cups" that can be used to protect sore nipples against irritation, and also to help draw out flat or inverted nipples. Nipple shields can be used to protect sore nipples while nursing. Consult a lactation consultant to see if these devices are appropriate for you.

WHAT TO DO FOR A DECREASED MILK SUPPLY

- Pump, Pump, Pump!!! Start immediately after feeding to let your body know more milk is required, and midway between feedings as needed.
- Always feed from both breasts and try to empty them. If your baby falls asleep and you are unable to empty both sides, then pump so your body knows it needs more milk.
- Do your best to stay calm: increased stress = decreased milk supply.
- Increase the frequency of nursing, especially if your milk supply has not fully come in yet.
- Drink lots of water, at least one big glass every time you nurse.
- Eat well-balanced and regular meals.

- Drink non-alcoholic beer – the hops really do help!
- Be aware that supplementing with formula can cause your milk supply to go down even more.
- Get as much rest as possible!

PUMPING

- If you need to pump, do it in the morning when your milk is most plentiful. Apply warm compresses for ten minutes prior to pumping.
- Get a double-electric breast pump (Medela) – it's worth every penny, it's fast and does the job well. You WILL use it!
- If you choose to use bottles in addition to nursing, try introducing one breastmilk bottle a day around week two or three, when milk has come in and nursing is well established. This is helpful to give yourself a break once in a while.
- It's okay to pump from one side and nurse from the other side.
- Look at picture of baby while pumping, to assist with milk let-down.
- After pumping, store your milk in good storage bags in the freezer, with the date labeled well. You can buy storage bags with handles and spouts for easy pouring – they work great! (www.onestepahead.com)
- Never use a microwave to warm or unthaw breastmilk. Microwaves can create "hot spots" in the milk that could burn baby's mouth, lower its vitamin C content, and can damage its anti-infective properties.

FOODS TO AVOID

- Cruciferous vegetables, which may cause baby to be gassy, such as cabbage, broccoli, cauliflower, beans, garlic, apricots, melon.
- Caffeine (coffee, tea, soda) and alcohol.

WEANING

- It can take anywhere from 1-2 weeks, and to up to a month to wean your baby to a bottle of formula or milk.

- Begin by adding 2 oz. mixed formula (if they're under 1 year) or milk (if they're over 1 year) to 6 oz. cup pumped breastmilk, to help them adjust to the taste of formula or milk. As you offer more bottles, slowly increase the amount of formula or milk and decrease the amount of breastmilk.

- Replace one feeding with a bottle for four to seven days, then replace two feedings for four to seven days, for example, until the baby is weaned.

- When you're giving a bottle, it is sometimes helpful to place a towel across your breasts so that the baby cannot smell breastmilk, or have someone else assist with the feeding.

- If your breasts become engorged, you can pump or manually express for the first one to three days, however avoid doing it longer as you will be tricking your body into thinking it needs to continue making more milk. If you experience discomfort, wear a very tight sports bra with ice packs.

Breast Milk Storage Guidelines

Fresh Breast Milk

- Room Temperature: 4 hours (77 degrees F/25 C), up to 10 hours (66-72 degrees F/19 C)
- Refrigerator: 3 days
- Freezer: 3 months in refrigerator freezer, 6 months in a deep freezer

Thawed Breast Milk

- Room Temperature: don't store at all
- Refrigerator: 24 hours
- Freezer: do not re-freeze

More Lifesavers

When Baby Cries

Living with a crying baby can be one of the most challenging times for a parent, especially if it persists for any length of time. Crying is normal; it's a baby's way of communicating their needs. However, when the crying follows a pattern it may be helpful to look into common causes to rule out a possible underlying medical condition.

RULE OUT CAUSES OF CRYING

- Is my baby hungry?
- Is my baby teething, sick, or gassy?
- Is my baby overtired? Over stimulated?
- Does the baby have a rash or uncomfortable clothing?
- Has there been a change in their routine?
- Is the room temperature comfortable?
- Are they bored or frustrated with something?
- How are the parents – are you frustrated?
- How are you holding the baby? Can you cuddle differently?
- Does your baby want to be rocked in a chair or swing for rhythmic soothing?

If you are not able to eliminate these typical culprits for crying, your baby may be experiencing colic. Always consult your doctor to rule out any other possible health issues. Your doctor will be the one to determine if your baby has colic.

DEFINITION OF COLIC
Continued crying or fussiness for three to four hours every day. Crying starts at the same time of day, most commonly in the evening. Colic usually starts in the first three weeks after birth and can last for three to four months.

Causes

It's not really known, but here are some theories:

- Milk allergy.
- Abdominal pain.
- Reflux.
- Studies have shown the temperament of your baby may trigger colic.
- Often times there is a diet/colic relationship. Try to keep feeding time quiet and relaxed. If you are feeding baby within 20 minutes, it's too fast.

If You Are Nursing

- Find out if there is something in your diet that is irritating your child.
- Eliminate milk and dairy products (including cheese and yogurt) from your diet.
- Avoid cruciferous vegetables (cabbage, broccoli, cauliflower, beans, garlic, apricots, and melon).
- Eliminate caffeine (coffee, tea, soda) and alcohol.

If You Are Bottle Feeding

- There are many different formulas available. Avoid switching from one formula to another, as your pediatrician should recommend which one is right for your baby.

How Parents Can Help

- Talk to your pediatrician about your concerns. Have a friend or family member entertain baby after exam so parent can discuss possible causes of crying with doctor undistracted.
- You cannot spoil your baby at this age! Try everything until you find something that works. Remember that what doesn't work one day may work the next.
- Reach out to family and friends for relief and support.
- Try to stay "cool" – walk out of the room for a few minutes and control your frustration. Do your best to react positively toward your baby.
- Sometimes just let them cry. Sometimes just let YOURSELF cry!
- Take fifteen minute shifts with your spouse when possible.
- Put the baby down! Let them cry for a little while so you can compose yourself.
- Remove cigarette smoke from the environment.
- Always remember you are a good parent and it WILL STOP.

Soothing Activities

- Stimulation encourages digestion, thus soothing an upset belly. With baby on their back, some good suggestions are:
  - ➡ rubbing belly in a clockwise circular motion
  - ➡ moving legs in bicycle motion
  - ➡ holding lower legs and move knees toward tummy, then out straight
- Burp baby frequently.
- Lay baby across your lap on their belly and rub their back.

- Try the "football hold" – carry your baby across your arm with face facing the floor, which puts pressure on belly and helps relieve gas while using a slight rocking motion.
- Turn on a hair dryer, dishwasher, vacuum cleaner, or washer/dryer as the continuous sound and vibration can be calming.
- Take a walk with baby.
- Rocking your baby in a rocking chair or cradle.
- Hold baby close and let them know they are loved.
- Hum and sing to baby.
- Swaddling in a blanket so baby feels cozy like in the womb.
- Play and offer the baby your undivided attention.
- Take a long drive in the car.
- Baby massage – classes are usually offered at local hospitals.
- Use an automatic swing, vibrating bouncy seat, or bounce them on your lap.
- Prepare a warm comforting bath with lavender.
- Apply a warm water bottle to tummy.
- Carry your baby in a front carrier, sling, or backpack.
- Offer a pacifier.
- When you change their diaper, leave clothes off for a while.

> Note that you should keep their head above belly at a 35-degree angle for sleep and after feedings, to aid digestion. You can put a blanket or pillow under the mattress to raise it on an angle.

Extras

- Gas drops.
- Automatic swings.
- Hot water bottle.
- Sound soothing machine with sounds of ocean waves and rain showers.
- Bottles designed to help reduce gas.

Colic always goes away!!!
Hang in there... this too shall pass!

Fill a sock with uncooked rice. Put it in the microwave for 30 seconds to one minute. Place it on baby's tummy; keep checking temperature of sock as rice continues to heat. It works as a little heating pad and the pressure feels good. You can reuse the rice sock over and over for months without refilling.

Sit and bounce on an exercise ball. It helps to calm the baby, while strengthening your abdominal muscles at the same time!

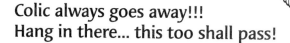

More Lifesavers

Sleep

The challenge of getting your baby to fall asleep – and keeping them there! – is probably not an issue you even considered before your first baby was born. With Norman Rockwell visions of a baby sleeping peacefully in a bassinet, you may come home from the hospital and find yourself pacing the halls night after night bouncing and singing, trying to get the little one to fall asleep. Unfortunately, this isn't where we can provide "this will solve it all" advice. There is no easy solution to give, as each child is different, and each unique situation requires its own remedy. We do have a few simple guidelines that may help to create a good sleeper, and give you some much needed rest too!

For the first few months, you cannot spoil your baby! Some believe the actual gestation period for a baby is actually "12" months, but is born at 9 months due to its size. So, the first three months they actually require a lot of closeness – swaddling, cuddling, and holding. Remember, your baby is used to being in a nicely controlled environment, one that is warm, with soothing noises, and calming massages. Then, they enter into a big, cold world and are trying to adjust. Babies need a lot of comforting attention, so do whatever it takes to soothe your baby and settle them to sleep.

However, after the first three to four months, one of the greatest gifts you can give your baby is the ability to soothe themselves to sleep. This will make napping and sleeping a more comfortable experience for baby and a LOT more peaceful for you! Around this age it is definitely time to start napping and bedtime routines. Babies will benefit from a ritual of bath, cuddling, story, and bed. Just remember to be wary of too many "associations" for falling asleep. If you have to have a feeding, rocking, music, a mobile, and a temperature of exactly 71.5 F to get them to sleep, then chances are they will require these things EVERY time. This may not be convenient for every nap or during the night as they move through their natural sleep cycles. YOU will be the one awake and providing these associations for them, and they will be uncomfortable at the inability to do it themselves.

It's a good idea to keep things simple – a nice little routine that you follow every night, with a "mini" routine for naps. Lay your baby down awake, and if they fall asleep while feeding, try to rouse them a little bit so they get used to settling themselves. It's also a good idea to choose a reasonable bedtime, such as 7:00-7:30 pm, and stick to it. If you wait until they're showing signs of tiredness, such as red eyes and irritability, you have probably passed their ideal bedtime and may have a harder time getting them to sleep because they are over-tired. You may have to let your baby cry – it's okay, and a common part of the journey of learning to self-soothe. If they cry, let them go for a few minutes, then enter the room and rub their backs, but don't pick them up. Leave again, and let them cry for another few minutes, repeating until baby is asleep. This may take several nights for them to "learn" to fall asleep themselves, but it will be worth every difficult moment of the process when you are able to just lay them down and walk away!

Sleep is an issue that is worthy of its own book, and there are great resources available, including:
- "Healthy Sleep Habits, Happy Baby" by Dr. Marc Weissbluth
- "Sleep: The Brazelton Way" by T. Berry Brazelton and Joshua D. Sparrow
- "Solve Your Child's Sleep Problems" by Richard Ferber
- "The No-Cry Sleep Solution: Gentle Ways to Help Your Baby Sleep Through the Night" by Elizabeth Pantley and William Sears M.D.

"Nothing compares to the wonder of small children when you are the light of their lives."

2 . CHILDCARE

Childcare Options

Returning to work after the birth of your baby can be a very emotional and difficult time. It can be very stressful to leave your child with a caregiver for the first time. If you are feeling anxious or uncertain, know that you are not alone! Be confident in yourself and the decision you made. Whatever your decision, know that you are making the best choice for you and your family.

Thankfully, childcare options have come a long way. Many regulatory and "watch dog" agencies are now in place to assess childcare environments and provide training and education to anyone working with children. There are also many different choices available to parents to fit your individual needs. Take the time to evaluate your needs honestly and research your options thoroughly. Doing this will help to ease your mind during the workday, and will ensure a good situation for everyone.

CHOOSING THE RIGHT CARE

- What kind of environment do we want for our child?
- Do we need a flexible care plan?
- How much can we afford to spend?
- Do we want our baby close to work?
- What size setting do we want?
- How convenient do we need the care to be?
- Do we want someone in our home on a daily basis?

Check out the National Network for Child Care at www.nncc.org for up to date resources about childcare.

NANNY

Advantages

- Child remains in the comfort of your home.
- Avoid hectic drop off and pick-up of your child.
- Not necessary to pack-up your child with supplies each day.
- Your child is not exposed to as many people or children, therefore decreasing the exposure to germs and illnesses.

- If agreed upon, the nanny can help with housekeeping tasks around the house allowing more "quality time" with your child at the end of the day.

Keep in Mind

- A good nanny agency will interview YOU, listen to your needs, and match you with potential candidates for you to interview.
- Make sure you give an honest, philosophical perspective on your family life, especially on discipline.
- These candidates affect the balance of your home life; you will want the nanny to meld into your family life harmoniously.
- Ask for a commitment that will suit your needs (six months, 1year).
- You must be selective and follow your instincts. If you feel like the candidates aren't the right match, keep searching. It's very disruptive to the family routine if you have to make a change soon into the job.
- Have a potential nanny come to your house and observe how they interact with the children. Look for politeness and respect for the mom, and joy and excitement with the kids.

- Many nanny services offer short term services for emergencies, such as illness or hospitalization of parent, or after the birth of successive children when you need an extra hand.

> **Ask yourself these questions as you interview:**
> - Who will mesh best with my child?
> - Do they have the experience and background I am comfortable with?
> - Is the candidate willing to adjust to our family dynamics?

HOME-BASED CHILD CARE

Advantages

- Tends to be the most affordable type of care in comparison to daycare centers and nanny services.
- Individual needs of children can be met well. For example, favorite foods can be offered, and potty training will remain consistent.
- The setting is intimate, while still providing social interaction with other children.
- Introduces your child to another home environment outside of their own.
- Your child's daily routines can be better maintained as compared to a daycare center.

Keep in Mind

- Ages of children in daycare are extremely important to be aware of, as it will be easier for the daycare provider if the children are closer together in age. Be sure that the provider will be able to provide the same amount of attention to older as well as younger children.
- Observe how the house is designed and ensure it is suitable for children.
- Is there a fenced in area outside?
- Are there too many stairs to maneuver?

- Is the home child-proof?
- Prepare a back-up plan if caregiver has to cancel, becomes ill, or goes on vacation.
- Many families like the intimacy of care for infants in this setting because it's most like home.

DAY CARE CENTER

Advantages

- Accredited centers will provide interaction with children and adults in an engaging educational atmosphere.
- Staff is trained in child development and safety procedures.
- Care is reliable even if a staff member is on vacation or ill.
- May provide a model of care that translates well as your child grows into a pre-school setting.
- Licensed centers are scrutinized and evaluated for safety and hygiene standards.

Keep in Mind

- Carefully observe the classrooms.
- Are the children active and engaged?
- Are caregivers attentive?
- Is it clean?
- Do they practice good hand washing habits? Are hand washing stations stocked with paper towels and hand washing liquid?
- Is the outside play area clean, organized, and safe? Does it have a variety of equipment?
- What are their policies if a child is sick?
- Is the center convenient to your home? Do they have an early drop off option?
- What is the late pick-up policy?
- What days are they closed (holidays)?
- Do they follow a similar work week to yours?

GENERAL ADVICE FOR HOME AND CENTER-BASED SETTINGS

Ask Questions!

- What are their credentials? If it's a daycare center, is it accredited?
- Are they licensed?
- What are the teacher to child ratios?
- How many children are there and what are their ages?
- When was the last social service check in?
- Is the facility a bright, happy place, well stocked with toys and engaging activities?
- Do they have an open door policy for parents?
- Look at the toys and art projects in the room – are they appropriate for your child's age and skill level?
- Do the children look engaged and happy?
- Is the staff or caregiver trained in child development?
- Does their philosophy match yours?
- Do they have a good reputation within the community?
- Ask for references and call them.

Tips

- Visit as many settings as possible.
- Be aware of ALL the hired help at a daycare, not just the person who owns or manages it.
- Talk to friends who have similar values and parenting styles for referrals.
- Observe the way your child behaves around the caregiver and follow your instincts.
- Be sure of an "open door policy" so you can drop in anytime unannounced.
- Visit a lot of providers and take a friend or spouse with you to get their feedback as well – they might notice things or ask questions that you don't.

More Lifesavers

Babysitting

Every family deserves a good, reliable babysitter! Make finding one a top priority, even before your baby is born. You will appreciate the freedom it gives you to stretch your wings every once in a while!

HOW TO FIND ONE

- Network with your family, friends and neighbors.
- Use children of friends whom you know and trust.
- Look for babysitting lists at the library.
- Inquire at your local high school.
- Nanny services often have college students available on weekends who desire some extra income.
- Try a job posting board at a local college in the education department.

PARENT RESPONSIBILITIES

- Try out any potential babysitters first as a mother's helper.
- Have the sitter "shadow" you for a half a day or so to gain knowledge about your child and family, where supplies are kept and the lay of the land.
- Treat your sitter with dignity and respect – after all, they are taking care or your precious children, and this is how you want them to treat your children.

- Pay them well! You want to provide continuity with your children, so having an eager and committed sitter will benefit all involved.
- Take the time to make your expectations clear regarding discipline, clean-up, how much you will pay, and when you will return.
- Be consistent with your schedule and away time. If you say you will be home at a specific time, adhere to that.
- Keep a list of household rules and routines handy.
- If your babysitter is not an adult, try to have an adult neighbor or parent of the sitter available in case of an emergency.
- Background checks can be done at your local police department.

> Create a laminated list of emergency numbers with magnetic adhesive strips on the back to keep on the refrigerator. Ensure the sitter is aware of how 911 works in your area. For example, are they required to provide the home address when calling?

More Lifesavers

_____

_____

_____

_____

_____

EMERGENCY INFORMATION SHEET

Home Address:

Home Phone Number:

Cell Phone Numbers:

Parent's Work Address and Work Number:

Parent's Work Address and Work Number:

Neighbor's Name and Number:

Neighbor's Name and Number:

Other Family Member's Name and Number:

Other Family Member's Name and Number:

Emergency: **9-1-1**

Police Department:

Fire Department:

Hospital:

Health Insurance Company:

Policy Holder's Name:

Group or Policy Number:

Pediatrician's Name, Number, and Address:

Dentist's Name, Number, and Address:

Poison Control Center:

Preschool

There are many preschool options available. If you decide to enroll your child in a preschool, consider what kind of learning and social environment best suits them. Being diligent in your search will help to ensure the best possible experience for these early learning years. A contributing factor to your decision may be the cost. Preschools are typically the parents' financial responsibility, although this varies between settings. While preschool open houses may be convenient for your inquiries, be sure to set up an appointment to observe the school in action. Observing the teachers and students interacting together will give you a feel for the flow of the program and the level of contentment of the children. It may also be helpful to have your child attend with you, so they can be active participants in your decision.

SOME GUIDELINES FOR THE SEARCH

- What is the philosophy of the preschool?
- What are the educational goals for each age group?
- How long is the school day and what days and schedules are available?
- How do they facilitate learning? Do they foster independence and community building?
- Is there a routine? What does it involve?
- Is there a safety protocol in place?
- Is it a balanced day of structured learning and free-choice play?
- Are children allowed to pursue activities that diverge from group activities?
- How are the children interacting with each other?
- What discipline technique is being used?
- How is the child's development evaluated and how is this communicated to the parents?
- Observe the environment carefully. Is there enough space? Does it look organized? Are materials appropriate and in good working order?
- Are the activities engaging and educationally interesting?
- Is the school prepared and sensitive to children that have transition anxiety and need a helping hand joining classroom activity?
- Is there a willingness to work with the family if issues arise?
- Your instincts should be a good indication. Would YOU feel comfortable and happy there?

HOW TO PREPARE YOUR CHILD FOR PRESCHOOL

- Prepare your child for their new experience. Share your thoughts and highlight the wonderful new adventure they are embarking on.
- Allow your child to have ownership of their school life. Take them on a shopping trip to buy a new backpack and some new clothes.
- Honor the first day and make it as stress-free as possible. Clear your schedule and allow extra time for the new transition.
- The first few days may go well with the initial separation. However, as the novelty wears off after week two or three, you may see some separation anxiety. Skilled teachers are aware of this. Communicate with your preschool to remedy any problems surrounding this issue.
- If your child is having a difficult time at drop-off, make sure they have the support of their teacher, who can help with this process.
- Ask your child questions about how the day went – let them know you care and are interested in how and what they are doing.
- Be open and allow your child to decompress from their day. Try not to over-schedule your child with after school activities, as they may be tired and need down time.

PRESCHOOL OPTIONS

Public Integrated Preschools – Children that qualify for special-needs services are often placed in the public school district's preschool. These preschools are specifically designed to integrate "typically" developing students with students that require special services in the classroom.

Private Preschools – There are several preschool environments, ranging from separate age groups meeting in individual classrooms, to groupings of children meeting in an open concept setting.

Religious-Based Preschools – Along with educational and social components, these schools incorporate religious education.

Headstart – Lower income families and single families may qualify for this publicly funded preschool program (www.nhsa.org).

Montessori – Created by Maria Montessori who believed "children learn from doing", this is a mixed age grouping of children who initiate their own learning, working with specially designed learning tools (www.amshq.org and www.montessor-ami.org).

For information about preschool accreditation and issues, visit the National Association for the Education of Young Children (NAEYC) serving children from birth to age 8 (www.naeyc.org).

More Lifesavers

"Childrearing is a JOURNEY,
not an EVENT – learning something
every day, every minute.
Children are the best gift you will
ever receive!"

3 . OUTWARD BOUND

Out and About

Gone are the days of zipping in and out of the mall, enjoying a peaceful and relaxing restaurant meal, and browsing through a favorite bookstore. Going out in public with children is a lot of work! Sometimes just the thought of packing everyone and everything up, loading the car and trudging through a store with unpredictable children is enough to make you stay at home. However, getting yourself outside and exposing your children to these adventures is extremely important in keeping everyone connected to the outside world. So read on, gain some make-it-easier advice, and JUST DO IT!

CHANGING AND FEEDING BABY

For Nursing

- If you are discreet you can usually facilitate nursing anywhere; a receiving blanket over the shoulder covers it all.
- Don't be afraid to breastfeed in public, but be sensitive to others around you who may not be as comfortable with nursing as you are.
- Wear loose, comfortable clothing for nursing on the go. Leave a spare shirt in the car for a quick change if needed.

For Bottle Feeding

- For formula, put boiling water in the bottle and bring pre-measured formula along (formula "singles" are handy). By the time you're ready to feed the baby, the water is usually at a good temperature and you don't have to worry about finding a place to heat the bottle. Or, take a small thermos of hot water and a small bottle of cold water so you can mix to the right temperature.
- Use liquid formula when going out so you don't have to worry about mixing water and powdered formula.

- If you have to heat a bottle, most restaurants or food courts will gladly give you a cup of hot water (ask for just a half a cup) to heat it up in.

General Tips

- Major department stores usually have a nice mothers' lounge that is very comfortable for nursing, changing diapers, and taking a break.
- A dressing room is a private place to feed your baby and change diapers.
- Try feeding your baby in the car between errands.
- Put pre-made bottles in a cooler bag with ice packs.
- Make sure your baby is fed and changed before you head home, so they won't melt down in the car.

> With your first child you will pack for a nuclear war – with your second you might grab a sippy cup and a diaper, and your third you will be begging someone else for a diaper!

PACKING THE DIAPER BAG

- Keep your handbag and diaper bag packed and ready to go at all times.
- It may be easier to use your pocketbook, bringing only the basics. Include two diapers, a small baggie of wipes, a small toy and you're good to go.

If you use a diaper bag, use a SMALL one. You don't need to pack enough supplies for a weekend trip for one morning at the mall or a visit to the doctor! Here is a list of suggestions:

- Two or three diapers.
- Small baggie of wipes.
- Disposable changing table cloths.
- Bottle and formula.
- Extra nursing pads.
- Burping cloth.
- Hand sanitizer gel.
- One small toy or rattle.
- For longer outings you may also want to add a spare set of clothing with a small bag to put dirty clothes into.

Remember that the more you bring, the more you have to carry!

General Tips

- If possible, bring help.
- Don't count on a perfect situation – be flexible with plans.
- Make it easy on yourself – plan on completing one errand only, and anything after that is a bonus.
- Time the outing according to baby's nap time – going for a walk with the stroller is good if its nap time, as they may sleep. Babies may or may not enjoy the stimulation of all the people, lights, and objects in a store.
- Bring snacks and sippy cups for toddlers.
- Always be prepared to sanitize with antibacterial lotion, gel, or wipes.
- For older children, have a "busy bag" ready to go for outings. It should be stocked with crayons, stickers, paper, small toys, and hard-covered books.
- "Buggy Boards" are great stroller attachments, so your older toddler or preschooler can "ride" along with you when they need a quick lift.
- NEVER give in to tantrums in public – it's a sure way of allowing it to happen again and again. Ignoring the tantrum and finishing your business as soon as possible will be effective if you do it consistently and with as little emotion as possible.
- Be prepared and willing to bail out if things aren't going well. Early exposure to outings is imperative in order to get baby acclimated to new environments.
- When parking your car on a hot day, have small blankets (receiving blankets work well) in the car to cover car seats. When you return to the car, the seats and buckles will not be too hot and uncomfortable for children to sit in.

DINING OUT

Restaurant Etiquette

- Make a reservation or use call-ahead seating if available. Always try to minimize the time your children will have to wait.
- If you have to wait, ask to look at a menu so you can order soon after you are seated.
- Choose restaurants that are kid-friendly with fast service.
- Booth seats keep kids more contained, and the baby carrier can be placed on the bench beside you.
- Don't let your child "wander" around a restaurant.
- Try going out to dinner late when the baby will be sleeping in the car seat. Ask for a highchair to turn upside down and set the seat into.
- Order food you know your children like. This isn't the time to introduce new foods, especially for picky eaters.
- Be courteous and make an attempt to clean excess food up off the floor (and if you aren't logistically able, drop a few bucks under the table for the person who has to clean it all up!).
- Tip very well if your children have made it a challenge for the wait staff, or if they have gone out of their way to make it easier for you.
- Remove children from restaurants for unruly behavior, and do not waiver – it's an effective way to teach consideration of others.

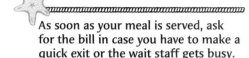

As soon as your meal is served, ask for the bill in case you have to make a quick exit or the wait staff gets busy.

Items to Bring

- Have a few ideas of games or activities you can play at the table to keep kids entertained before the food arrives, such as coloring book and crayons, a book to read, or a quiet toy that is fun to play with on a table top, such as "Wikki-stix".
- Bring wipes for hands before, during, and after meal.
- Disposable placemats that stick to the table are great! You can put food directly on the placemat and not worry about germs from the table, or glass dishes that may end up on the floor.
- Use disposable bibs or bring a bib clip (www.onestepahead.com).
- Most restaurants have only adult cutlery, so bring a small spoon and fork along.
- Using your own sippy cup will avoid spilled drinks.
- Bring your own baby food when possible, as little baby jars of food can be heated up for you.
- Know that eating in public is not a known skill – young children need plenty of practice to handle this VERY demanding task. If at first you don't succeed – keep trying. Be sure you're not expecting too much of your child – 30 minutes is a good length of time to have them sitting in public and behaving.

More Lifesavers

Grocery Shopping

While grocery shopping with children can be a fun activity, it can sometimes be a nightmare. Here are some suggestions to assist in making it a positive and successful outing.

STRATEGIES

- Always shop with a list. Organize it based on the food location in the store, to avoid jumping from aisle to aisle.

- Always have children use bathroom or change their diaper before going to the store.

- Before leaving, remove large items from the rear or trunk of car so you have room for the groceries.

- Explain your expectations to your children in the car before entering the store, and offer some sort of incentive for good behavior, such as picking out the fruit.

- There may be a few months when shopping with your children is more trouble than it's worth. Try to go when you have some help, or when they can stay at home.

- If possible, make it a family event, where child can play in cart with daddy pushing and mommy shopping. It makes a chore something to look forward to.

- Treat the experience as an educational opportunity – count out fruits and vegetables, teach about healthy foods and snacks.

- Try not to give in when children ask for something that you don't want to buy, as they will never learn the word "no" and you'll have lots of problems with subsequent shopping trips.

- Never go when you or your child is hungry.

- Shop at wholesale clubs, such as Sam's Club, Costco, and BJ's. It's cheaper, you can buy in bulk, and they give out samples!

When you first arrive home with a new baby, or anytime you get swamped, try a grocery delivery service if it's available in your town.

Once You're There...

- Find a grocery store with mini-cars attached to the cart to keep toddlers amused.

- Some grocery stores have miniature carts for children to push and follow the parent.

- Use a handy fabric cover for your shopping cart, such as the "Clean Shopper Shopping Cart Cover" to protect your child from germs.

- Bring sanitizer wipes to disinfect the handle and sides of the grocery cart.

- Use a baby backpack for hands-free shopping and avoid germ-infested carts.

- Keep child strapped in the carriage with a snack. Don't hesitate to open a package of crackers in the store if needed.

- Most stores will offer kids a piece of deli cheese at the beginning. Visit the bakery for a cookie at the end of the trip if they have been well behaved.

- Give kids jobs to do, such as counting fruits and vegetables as they are put into the produce bags, or if they are old enough, retrieving a few items from the shelves. The time will go by more quickly if they have something to focus on.

- Pick up the most important items first, in case you have to leave in a hurry.

- Don't be afraid to leave the whole cart of groceries and exit the store if things are not going well.

- Try to find a checkout aisle without candy.

Waiting... Waiting... Waiting...

Wherever you go or whatever you do, waiting is inevitable. While difficult enough when you're by yourself, with young children to control and entertain it can be extremely frustrating. The key is to be prepared at all times for both the expected and the unexpected "waits". A good lesson to remind ourselves and our children is: Patience is a Virtue!

CREATIVE TACTICS

- Schedule doctors' appointments first thing in the morning or right after lunch, as there will likely be less waiting if you're the first one. Late-morning and late-afternoon appointments are usually when the doctor is backed up and you have to wait.

- At the doctor's office, take stickers or crayons for them to use with the paper on the examining table. You can outline your child's body, and then have them draw on the face and clothes.

- Keep a small pad of paper and some stickers on hand.

- Play simple games such as "I Spy," "I'm thinking of…," treasure hunt, finger plays, word games, rhymes, singing, counting, spelling or math games, and tic-tac-toe.

- Don't be afraid to be silly. If YOU play, everyone has fun.

- Keep a small toy they haven't seen before in your bag, and pull it out when they've hit the wall!

- Have small books on hand to read or ask them to tell you a story.

- Use bribery! Be sure to follow up with your promise.

- Take this time to talk and visit with your child.

- Make sure your children are as comfortable as possible, bundling them up if it's cold, or stripping off outerwear if it's warm.

- Dump things out of your purse or diaper bag, and have child put it all back in.

- Take walks and keep kids distracted.

- Give them a whole apple (if they're old enough) – it takes a long time to eat!

- If you anticipate a wait, bring a "busy bag" of small toys and games.

- Start teaching your children about patience at an early age, even babies!

Call ahead to see if the doctor is running behind; some offices will tell you to come in a little later. Or, when you arrive ask if you can walk around outside for a bit if the doctor is running late – be sure to find out exactly when you should come back, and don't be a second late.

More Lifesavers

Travel

Traveling with infants and young children can seem like a daunting task. However, once you are organized and in the right mind-set, you will be off to make family memories of a lifetime!

OVERALL ADVICE

- Before you visit your travel destination, collect information about the location and things to do. Have each family member choose their top picks of things to do, so everyone feels included in the vacation plans.

- If you are planning to travel abroad, be sure to check with the countries you will be traveling to for any special vaccinations that may be needed. Also, you may want to avoid using tap water while abroad. Purchase reputable bottled water upon arrival.

- Travel to child-friendly places – do yourself a favor and make it a fun and positive experience for all to enjoy.

- Try to stay on your normal routine if possible. Keep naps consistent and sightsee when you know your children will be at their best. For example, go on a morning outing and spend the afternoon relaxing on the beach.

- Limit sightseeing and keep plans as simple as possible to get the most out of your trip. You and your children will be happier!

- Expect unforeseen events along the way that may complicate your plans, and be flexible.

- Roll clothing into outfits, including socks and underwear; pack two outfits a day for infants and toddlers.

- Be prepared to re-establish routines and sleeping patterns when you return from your trip. Don't worry – things will soon return to normal.

- Have fun! Trips away from home are a way to bond as a family and make lasting memories.

> Don't forget the fun of being a tourist in your own community! Jot down ideas of things to do when they come to mind and keep it handy for last minute excursions.

HELPFUL TRAVEL ITEMS

- A bag of NEW and interesting small toys always makes a trip easier.

- Have favorite snacks and non-perishable food on hand. Stock up on bottled water and juice boxes.

- Bring a stroller that is lightweight and easy to maneuver.

- Bring a first-aid kit that includes a pain reliever and cold medicine.

- DVD recorder for instant DVD's of your vacation.

- Keep a supply of different sized Ziploc baggies. You will be surprised at how convenient they are for wet clothes, trash, dividing up snacks, and playing games.

- Bring a stain remover stick or Shout Wipes to apply to stains, and spot clean when necessary.

- Pack 'n Plays are great for sleeping, and easy to transport.

- Quick and easy inflatable travel beds with electric pump are perfect for sleepovers to family and friends.

- If you use a sound machine at home when your baby sleeps, bring it with you on trips as this creates continuity in the sleep routine.

- Bring something familiar to assist with bedtimes, such as a favorite animal, pillowcase, a flannel sheet or nightlight.

WHEN IN THE CAR

Helpful Items

- Provide all the comforts your child will need on the trip including snacks, drinks, and pacifiers close by.
- Keep a small supply of good car toys, such as books and quiet toys without many pieces.
- Have a place to put garbage. On long car trips, throw out trash at every stop.
- Have a container of wipes available for quick clean-ups and sticky fingers.
- Keep emergency supplies in your vehicle, including a car emergency kit, blanket, and first-aid kit.
- Use a mirror that attaches to your rear view mirror to see the kids behind you.

Keep a port-a-potty in the trunk with small trash bags and wipes. Avoid spills by placing a few sheets of paper towels in the bottom of the potty to soak up urine until it can be disposed of properly.

How to Make it Bearable...and Enjoyable

- Books on tape or CD – make sure they are stories you enjoy listening to!
- Record your own favorite books on tape.
- Read out loud; make up your own stories.
- Sing-a-longs.
- Play games such as counting cars, I-Spy, guessing, and alphabet games.
- Bring pillows for the older children to prop up their neck and head.
- A portable DVD or VCR to watch movies for long car rides. Organize DVD's and CD's in a portable sleeve for quick access.
- Put home movies on video or DVD and enjoy family time in the car remembering fun times caught on tape.
- Crayola's "Travel Turtle Lap Desk" (www.misterart.com) is great for kids to color on.
- "I pods" are great to keep all your favorite family music organized and accessible.

- If you're traveling by yourself, keep a cooler on the front seat with you for snacks and drinks, so you can easily pass things to the back seat.
- "Colorforms" which stick to the car windows for a fun and easy diversion.

Car Travel Tips

- Secure heavy items in rear to avoid dangerous projectiles if you need to stop in a hurry or are in an accident.
- Prepare a small reward or treat incentive after a long car drive.
- Travel when it's good timing for your kids; if they sleep well in the car, then traveling at night can be very convenient and less stressful. Leaving at 4 or 5 in the morning for long trips is also nice because kids can get a few hours of sleep in before breakfast.
- Leave yourself enough time to stop, run, and stretch.
- If you're nursing during a long car trip, get a car adaptor for the breast pump and bring one pre-pumped bottle. Feed the first bottle with baby in car seat, then pump – the pumped bottle will keep until the next feeding. Bring bottled water to rinse the bottle after feeding.
- If you or your children suffer from motion sickness, ask for medication from your doctor ahead of time. Driving on an empty stomach sometimes exacerbates a sick tummy.

TRAVEL BY PLANE

Prior to Departure

- Book non-stop flights whenever possible.
- If possible, buy your child a ticket even if they're under two, as the extra space is always helpful.
- When booking a flight, try to be realistic about your child's routine. Fly when you know they are at their best.
- Rent car seats with the rental car so that you don't need to lug them through the airport.

- Skycap your luggage curbside, if one is available. If you are bringing a car seat, a carrying case is helpful to get to and from the gate.
- Instead of a purse, wear a backpack so your hands are free with passport, driver's license and tickets close at hand.
- Let your child carry a small backpack that THEY pack with comfort items, like their blanket and small favorite toys.

Lift Off

- If you are traveling alone with young children, pre-board if possible so you are guaranteed plenty of room in the overhead storage bin. The flight attendants will be able to assist you.
- Ask if you can gate-check your stroller on the jet way, or take your umbrella stroller on-board and stow it in the overhead compartment.
- Be sure to introduce yourself to flight attendants – they will become your best friends!
- Ask a flight attendant for pillows, blankets, cards, or kids' activity packs early before they run out of supplies.
- Bring extra food or formula, as you never know what kind of delays your plane will experience.
- To avoid ear pain, have baby nurse, drink a bottle, or suck on pacifier during take-off AND landing. Older kids can chew or drink, or "Earplanes" earplugs work well to equalize ears.
- Invest in a portable DVD player with child-size earphones.
- Bring easy snacks and drinks with lids. Beware of air pressure and the opening of beverages, as they could overflow.
- Good activities to bring along include coloring books and crayons, Color Wonder markers with paper, and NEW small toys.
- Bring wipes and large Ziploc bags for trash.

If you are traveling with a companion, have them board first to set-up and organize your possessions before children board to ease arrival onto the plane.

HOTEL AND RESORT STAYS

- Kid-friendly hotels will make life a lot easier whether you're on the road or on vacation. Look for amenities such as a babysitting service, restaurant, room service, laundry facilities, pool, kitchenettes, and mini-store for forgotten supplies.
- Check if accommodations offer "family rates".
- If possible, reserve a room away from the elevator or stairway to avoid excess noise.
- Some resorts will provide a mini-fridge in your room for a minimal cost.
- Reserve a crib, extra cot, or bedrails ahead of time.

VISITS TO FAMILY OR FRIENDS

- See if your host can borrow items for you such as a stroller, car seat, Pack 'n Play and highchair.
- It's helpful if your host can shop for the essentials before you arrive (diapers, wipes, formula) so you don't have to carry everything with you, or rush out to the store upon arrival.
- Do not depend on others to have what you need for your children. If there is something important that your child needs then bring it with you.
- Grocery shop yourself when you arrive to ensure you'll have foods available that your children enjoy.
- Inform your hosts of foods your children prefer, to make mealtimes easier.
- Make sure there are plenty of things for the kids to do, even if you need to bring your own toys.
- Be a gracious guest; always bring a small token of appreciation for the host.

Life's a Beach

A favorite summer pastime for many families is heading to the beach! Whether it's the ocean, a lake, a pond, or an old swimming hole, most children love the water! Before your outing begins, check out this array of tried-and-true supplies that may help to make the trip more comfortable and fun. And of course, keep in mind the important safety considerations as well.

HELPFUL SUPPLIES FOR THE KIDS

- Extra bathing suit or clothing.
- Swim diapers.
- Hats ("Flap Happy" brand makes comfortable ones that stay on infants and toddlers).
- Swim shoes.
- Child sized towels and terry cloth cover-ups.
- Mesh bag with sand toys.
- Safety flotation devices.
- Portable crib for the tiny ones.
- Infant or family cabanas are wonderful for babies to rest in and mothers to nurse in, providing excellent sun protection and privacy.

HELPFUL SUPPLIES FOR EVERYONE

- "Beach Deluxe Wonder Wheeler" is great to transport all your supplies (www.leapsandbounds.com).
- Sun block. The continuous spray is the easiest to use and re-apply to bodies and the "stick" type is the easiest to apply to toddlers and preschoolers faces.
- Sunglasses.
- Lightweight beach chairs.
- Umbrella.
- Cooler.
- Insect repellent.
- Disposable waterproof camera.
- Trash bags and wipes.

BEFORE YOU HIT THE BEACH

- Be very alert with your children around any water source. Even if there is a lifeguard on duty it doesn't mean you can let YOUR guard down...always have your eye on your children.
- Be conscious of rip currents. The National Weather Service has great information about this hazard, check it out before you head to the beach.
- The invisible UV-rays are harmful to children's delicate skin; therefore burns can occur even on cloudy or hazy days without protection.
- The sun is brightest from 10am to 2pm; reapply sunscreen often and after every splash in the water!
- UV rays reflect off of sand, water, and grass. You are not necessarily safe in shade – don't stay out too long.
- Be aware that serious skin conditions are caused by radiation damage that occurs during childhood, and that more than half of a lifetime's sun exposure occurs during this time.
- Heat stroke can occur if children are out in the sun too long or over dressed on a warm day. Body temperatures may rise significantly (over 105 degrees Fahrenheit) and require immediate medical attention, so keep well hydrated.

> Put sunscreen on 30-60 minutes before you venture outside. Check with your pediatrician regarding putting sunscreen on infants under 6 months old. Older children should start with an SPF of no less than 30. Keep in mind that sunscreen usually expires after a year.

"Follow your instincts about what you think is 'normal' for development. If you think something is 'not quite right', don't stop asking questions and looking for answers until you are satisfied."

Teething and Tooth Care

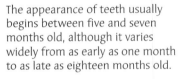

The little chiclets that poke out of your baby's and toddler's gums look so adorable! However, the process of exposing themselves can be quite a journey. Our little cherubs may display symptoms of a common cold or an ear infection, when in fact their teeth are fighting to burst forth. This process, so vital and necessary, may for some children be uncomfortable. Arming yourself with the knowledge of teething and solutions to alleviate the discomfort will make it a much easier process…for both of you.

Teething 411

The appearance of teeth usually begins between five and seven months old, although it varies widely from as early as one month to as late as eighteen months old.

Typically, the bottom two front teeth emerge first, followed by the top four front teeth. Next, the two flanking teeth adjacent to the two bottom front, followed by the back molars, and finally the eye teeth (the pointy teeth in the upper jaw).

Your child will have twenty teeth by the time they are three years old.

SIGNS THAT BABY IS TEETHING

"Teething" actually begins before the teeth emerge, sometimes making it difficult to know if the process has begun or not. Here are some clues that it may be starting:

- Child pulls at jaw or ears.
- Increased fussiness for no obvious reason.
- Excessive drooling and chewing on things.
- Waking at night with fussiness and crying.
- Gums appear red, tender, or sore.
- May refuse solids or bottles due to increased pressure on gums.
- Possibly a low-grade fever. If baby has a high fever, this is NOT due to teething and medical attention is required.

WAYS TO RELIEVE TEETHING PAIN

- Cold teething rings.
- Slightly thawed frozen bagels or teething biscuits, such as Zwieback.
- Natural teething gel, or Hyland's Homeopathic teething tablets. *(Hint: dissolve the tablets in a teaspoon of water and use a medicine dropper to give to babies.)*
- Limited amounts of infant acetaminophen or ibuprofen (may help baby sleep better).
- Gently massage swollen gums with a clean finger or gauze.
- Sugar-free or all-natural juice freezies or popsicles (ages 1 and up).
- Cold, wet washcloths fresh from the fridge or freezer to chew on.

BRUSHING THE PEARLS

- Around two months, start massaging baby's gums with a piece of gauze. This helps toughen them to prepare for teething.

- As the first tooth emerges, brush lightly with a cloth or soft infant toothbrush and water.

- At 15 months, (check with your pediatrician) begin using a very small amount of regular children's toothpaste, encouraging spitting and rinsing. Teach them not to swallow the toothpaste.

- Brush their teeth yourself first to ensure a proper cleaning, and then allow them to hold the brush and do it themselves.

- Instill good habits early – always supervise tooth brushing sessions to make certain teeth are being cleaned thoroughly. Taking care of baby teeth is equally as important as the adult teeth!

- Don't forget to assist with your child's daily flossing.

- Never put baby to bed with a bottle, as it can contribute to tooth decay.

- Don't feed your child 2 hours prior to a dentist visit as a sensitive gag reflex may induce vomiting.

MAKING IT FUN

- Character toothbrushes with large handles.

- "Spin brushes" that make cool whirring sounds.

- Toothbrushes that light up for one minute.

- Kid-friendly flavors of toothpaste.

- Timers that buzz after one minute of brushing.

- Character themed dental flossers.

- Fun small cups for rinsing.

A NOTE ON FLUORIDE

Fluoride has proven cavity-fighting properties, and is necessary for children. Small, pea-sized amounts help to strengthen tooth enamel and decrease the risk of cavities. However, large amounts can cause permanent teeth stains. Monitor your children for swallowing of toothpaste while brushing, and store paste out of reach. Tap water is a good source of fluoride, and for those who have water that is not fluoridated, check with your pediatrician to see if supplements are needed, usually at six months of age.

FINDING A GOOD DENTIST

- Children typically begin seeing a dentist around age three, with visits every six months. Your pediatrician will monitor for any tooth problems, and will recommend an earlier visit if needed.

- Find a great dentist early as some have waiting lists. Locate one who specializes in pediatric dentistry and has a pleasant and gentle manner with children.

- Ask around – if a friend or family adores their dentist, try that practice.

- Contact your insurance company, or your pediatrician for referrals.

- The effort to find a caring, sensitive, and fun dentist is crucial to making appointments less intimidating and more enjoyable.

- For further assistance locating a pediatric dentist in your area, visit www.aapd.org, the website of the American Academy of Pediatric Dentistry.

Weaning from Pacifiers and Bottles

Pacifiers and bottles can become an extension of a child's body if you let them, and removing these items can feel like removing a limb! Children use these objects to satisfy a need. Be ready and willing as a parent to "give it up" because half the battle often lies with the parents and their willingness to forgo a few peaceful nights for the ultimate challenge of weaning. You are in charge of this transition, and your child needs YOU to be strong! Hopefully the following tips will provide useful suggestions, and some moral support, to help make this challenging time a little easier.

GENERAL WEANING TIPS

- Don't plan to get rid of these comfort objects or behaviors until you are REALLY ready. If you give up half way through, your child may remember that you gave in, and will try even harder the next time to get you to give in.

- Choose a toy your child really wants to have. Make a sticker chart, and as soon as they go ten days without using the pacifier or bottle, they earn the toy. Keep it on display where they can see but not reach it.

- Set a "rite of passage" date. Tell your child that on a certain day, for example their second or third birthday, the pacifier or bottle will be stopped. Give your child lots of forewarning, and talk about it so they are clear on what will happen. Stick to it – it may be rough for one or two days, but they'll get over it.

- Divert their attention by substituting a favorite toy or giving them your attention instead!

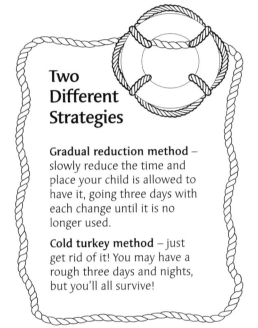

Two Different Strategies

Gradual reduction method – slowly reduce the time and place your child is allowed to have it, going three days with each change until it is no longer used.

Cold turkey method – just get rid of it! You may have a rough three days and nights, but you'll all survive!

BOTTLES

- Start using a sippy cup around six months; at least offer it to them to try.
- Don't put anything in a bottle besides milk.
- Feed baby BEFORE bedtime, so they're not relying on it for comfort to get themselves to sleep.
- Eliminate one bottle at a time.
- Try using Avent bottles and sippy cups. The nipple fits on the sippy cups, making a nice transition from bottle to cup.
- Put a brand new liquid in the cup. It's preferable to put whole milk in the cup and reserve formula or breast milk for the bottle.
- Put ice cubes in the cup – kids love the sound of the rattle.
- Use a reward system, such as a sticker chart for each time they forego a bottle.

PACIFIERS

- Extended, heavy use of pacifiers may contribute to speech and language difficulties, and may cause problems with teeth.

- If you keep them limited to naps and bedtime ONLY from day one, it will make it much easier to wean them later.
- Make the pacifier uninviting for use. Rough the pacifier up with sandpaper or cut the tip off.
- Try dipping it in pickle juice for an unsavory suck…they will give it up right there on the spot!

THE "BREAK-UP"

- Have a "Bye-Bye Pacifier" party and let your child pick out a toy to replace it. Have friends over for cupcakes.
- "Mail" the pacifier to one of your children's favorite characters, such as Mickey Mouse or Dora, and write a letter back expressing pride in their choice.
- Have the "Pacifier Fairy" come and take the pacifier away during the night, leaving a present in its place.
- Take your child to a Build-a-Bear Workshop and when making the bear have your child place the pacifier inside. This way they can still "sleep" with it!
- Have your child trade it in for a desired toy.
- Enlist the help of your dentist or pediatrician. Have them present the coveted reward in exchange for the bottle or pacifier.

More Lifesavers

Constipation

Before you had children you probably swore you would never be one of those parents who talks about their child's bowel movements. Then sure enough one day, you find yourself sitting at a gathering of friends indeed discussing all the ins and outs – color, size, consistency, and smell! What enters and what leaves a child's body is certainly important to their overall health. Any difficulties with constipation should be discussed with your pediatrician and with friends who have also dealt with the same problems. Here is a brief outline of the issue, and some suggestions as to what you can do about it. Constipation IS worthy of conversation – just not around the table, please!

IS YOUR CHILD CONSTIPATED?

Bowel habits vary amongst children, sometimes making it difficult to tell if your child is truly constipated. Following are some signs to watch for:

- With a newborn, stools less than once every two days.
- With older children, stools that are dry and hard. Some children can go every five to seven days with soft stools and this is normal.
- At any age, hard stools that are painful to eliminate.
- Abdominal pain that is relieved by a bowel movement.
- Blood in, or on the outside of, the stool.
- Small amounts of soiling between movements.

POTENTIAL CAUSES

- A diet low in fiber.
- Not drinking enough water.
- Drinking too much milk, greater than 12-16 ounces per day.
- Waiting too long to go to the bathroom.
- Certain medications.
- Toddlers being toilet-trained who purposefully "hold it in" to avoid going.

TO HELP INFANTS

1. Increase Fluids

- Give 2-4 oz. of water or diluted fruit juices (such as apple or pear) 1-2 times a day. Try adding 1/2 tsp. of prune juice to formula.

2. Increase Fiber

- If over 4 months old, try high-fiber foods such as cereals, strained prunes, apricots, or spinach.

Remember That...

- Constipation is uncommon in breastfed infants since breastmilk is so easily digested.
- It is common for a baby to have a bowel movement only every one to two days.
- If stools are soft or watery, then it is not constipation, even if it is infrequent.
- It is common for both nursing and formula-fed infants to strain or groan when having a bowel movement, due to weak abdominal muscles.
- Iron in formula does not cause constipation, so don't switch to a low-iron or soy formula without a doctor's recommendation.

TO HELP TODDLERS AND CHILDREN

1. Increase Fluids

- Increase the amount of water they are drinking to a minimum of two to three glasses per day.
- If your child doesn't like drinking water, flavor it with a little juice (not more than 12 ounces a day), or try flavored waters.

2. Increase Fiber

- Give enough grams of fiber to equal your child's age, plus 5, each day. For example, a 2 year old = 7 g/day, 4 years old = 9 g/day.

How to Increase Fiber in the Diet

Getting more fiber into your children's diet is easier than you think:

- Check the fiber content on everything you eat. High fiber foods have at least 3-4 g of fiber per serving.
- Buy organic and health food products which often have more fiber in them and less sugar. Try brands such as Barbara's and Kashi.
- Add whole grains to your baking. Try using more whole wheat flour and rolled oats (not instant).
- Use whole wheat breads and pastas.
- Increase bran in cereals and muffins.
- Serve oatmeal or shredded wheat for breakfast.
- Popcorn is a great high-fiber snack.
- Introduce pear or prune juice. They can be a little thick, but some kids really like it because of the sweetness, and you can easily mix it with water or other juices.
- Helpful hint: if they won't drink prune juice, try disguising it in a different bottle. Tell them it's "medicine" and give it to them in a medicine dropper or syringe several times a day.
- Serve more fruits: apples, pears, prunes, apricots, figs, plums, raisins, cantaloupe, strawberries, raspberries, peaches, cherries.
- Serve more vegetables: beans (green, kidney, pinto), peas, broccoli, sweet potatoes, turnips, raw tomatoes, corn, lettuce, carrots.

Sprinkle wheat germ on as many of their foods as you can, such as spaghetti, meatloaf, hamburgers, pancakes, cereal, or toast – they won't even notice! You can also put it in an actual "sprinkles" bottle and let the kids do it themselves.

3. Decrease Constipating Foods

- Avoid constipating foods such as cow's milk, cheese, bananas, peanut butter, and rice.
- Try to figure out what foods may be giving your children problems, and cut them out until things are moving smoothly, then re-introduce small amounts.

4. Medication

- ONLY with a doctor's recommendation. Ask about Little Tummy's Laxative Drops, a natural vegetable senna formula.

5. Get More Exercise

- Take your children for a short walk each day, or let them run and play in the backyard.
- Enroll them in activities that promote exercise, such as dance, swimming, gymnastics.
- Play a children's exercise or dance video, such as Sesame Street's "Happy Healthy Monsters" or "Yoga Kids."

6. Strategies

- Be patient with your child, as constipation is a chronic problem that takes time to improve.
- Encourage child to have regular bowel movements. Try having them sit on the toilet following meals.
- Use a simple rewards system or a daily calendar with stars or stickers for days that your child eats and drinks well, and has a bowel movement.

> **REMINDER** Visit your pediatrician if the measures you have taken do not work to solve the problem.

Potty Training

Another one of the big questions on the playground is, "Is your toddler potty trained?" It's a sometimes dreaded question – almost as personal as your favorite presidential candidate! Understanding that potty training is an emotional milestone, more so than a physical one, will ease your burden. Remain positive and consistent when your child begins this huge undertaking. Lots of praise will encourage the process.

ARE YOU READY?

- Do you have the necessary equipment, such as a potty seat, reading material and soft wipes?
- Are you prepared to be patient and flexible?
- Is the whole family on board to assist?
- Are you prepared to invest the TIME and CONSISTENCY needed?

IS YOUR CHILD READY?

- Do they seem interested in using the potty?
- Can they pull up their pants?
- Do they like being in the bathroom?
- Does your child dislike being wet or soiled?
- Does your child communicate their need to go to the bathroom?
- Can your child follow simple instructions?

HELPFUL PRODUCTS

- The potty seat by Baby Bjorn is a good one because it is easy to clean and comes in fun colors.
- Get a special, soft, contoured seat for your toilet. If your child will sit on the real toilet, then you don't have a small potty to empty and clean. If your child can't reach the toilet, get a small stool.
- Put Cheerios in the toilet for boys to aim at.
- Put some children's books or magazines in the book rack.
- Read the "Once Upon a Potty" book and video. The song is great!

- Use a kids' foam pump soap – it's fun, easy to use, and smells great. You can also easily tell if your kids washed their hands!
- Use flushable kids' wipes so kids can independently wipe themselves. Establish habit of wiping front to back.
- Diapers or pull-ups that "feel wetter" so child knows when they're wet.
- "Piddle Pads" are great to help protect your car seat in case of an accident.
- If you're potty training an older child, bring a portable toilet seat which folds up small enough for a diaper bag which you place over the larger seats often found in public restrooms. Available at www.onestepahead.com.

Put blue food coloring in the toilet – when the kids pee, it turns the water green!

STRATEGIES

Before you Begin

- If they don't understand the words associated with it, don't even start trying.
- Wait until they are ready, generally age three for boys and two for girls. This will decrease stress and frustration and help to ensure success.
- As a parent, you have to listen to your child's needs and assess if they are indeed ready. If so, begin the process in a sensitive and consistent manner.
- Boys tend to accomplish toileting several months after girls.

Ready, Set, GO

- Have your child observe another child or parent using the potty.

- Let them go without diapers and pants, and keep them outside or in an area of your house that is hardwood or tile. This way, they can start connecting the need and urge to go with what it feels like to "go". Be ready with lots of paper towels!

- Keep child naked from the waist down. Carry the potty chair to whatever room the child is in. When they start peeing on floor, quickly place them on potty and tell them they must pee in there. Do this EVERY time. You will need to make this your full-time project until they get it.

- Use a reward chart. Every time your child tries to use the potty they receive a sticker. When four or five stickers are earned they receive a small treat.

- Give high praise when they initiate even sitting on the potty.

- Make sure they are dried immediately after an accident so they see how much better it feels.

- Make a big deal about how proud of themselves they should be.

- Tell your child they will get a very special visitor when they're potty-trained, and then have someone come over, dressed like a Cinderella or another favorite character.

- Promise a special phone call from "Dora" or "Bob the Builder", and have a friend call to tell them what a great job they're doing.

- Train your child in the warm summer months when they'll be unencumbered by lots of clothing.

- Celebrate the simple accomplishments, such as pulling up a pull-up, lifting potty lid, and flushing.

- Most of, all don't push them too hard. Relax – they won't go to college in diapers!

- Once your child has conquered the "peeing part", remember that bowel movements often take one to three months longer…bummer!

Go camping! When ready, take them camping for a week. Since there is a lot of peeing outdoors or using the potty chair in the tent, there will be less accidents and a bit more focus on the process itself. The child also has the benefit of seeing the adults make a conscious effort to use the bathrooms at the campsite. When you return home, using the bathroom will seem easy!

NIGHTTIME POTTY TRAINING TIPS

Keeping dry during the night is usually the last phase of toilet training. This can occur as early as age three, or as late as ages five or six, and most often later in boys than girls. A hormonal change is required in order for children to keep themselves dry through the night. So be patient and don't put pressure on your child, as they have little control over it. If they surpass age 6 or are bothered by the nighttime wetting, consult your pediatrician.

- Always remain positive with your child, as this process often takes longer than daytime training.

- Do not allow them to take drinks to bed.

- Switch to pull-ups so the child "feels" wet.

- Try placing a potty seat in their bedroom to avoid nighttime wandering and accidents along the way.

- Use a full length, water absorbing mattress cover. If you use two of them (one placed on top of the other), you can simply remove the top one during the night if your child has an accident.

- Keep extra pajamas and sheets nearby for quick night changes.

- If child has access to the bathroom at night, make sure the pathway is well lit.

- Continue using praise and positive feedback.

_____ 's

Potty Chart

ONE STICKER PER TRY ON POTTY

Monday [ ] [ ] [ ] [ ] REWARD

Tuesday [ ] [ ] [ ] [ ] REWARD

Wednesday [ ] [ ] [ ] [ ] REWARD

Thursday [ ] [ ] [ ] [ ] REWARD

Friday [ ] [ ] [ ] [ ] REWARD

Saturday [ ] [ ] [ ] [ ] REWARD

Sunday [ ] [ ] [ ] [ ] REWARD

Routines and Transitions

From infancy onward, predictable routines are valuable to a child's day. Guided by actions within the home environment, routines are important in helping your children anticipate events that occur habitually throughout the day. Not only do routines help children feel safe and assured, it can help to develop cognitive skills, such as attention and memory. Just as an adult gauges time with a clock, children need routines to gauge time during the day.

Routines facilitate transitions from one activity to the next, such as from breakfast to getting dressed, or leaving a playground to go home. Transitions with children can be one of the more tricky parenting skills to accomplish. Even if your lifestyle doesn't allow for "strict" routines, having some reliable structure to the day will help your children feel secure. Once family routines are established, do what you can to stick to them, as consistency keeps children feeling grounded – and mothers feeling sane!

ROUTINES

Approaches

- Begin to set expectations early in your child's life.
- Kids need boundaries, and parents need to provide that for them. They will naturally push the limits and it's up to a parent to enforce the routine, even if chaos ensues.
- Children mirror their parents. Be a good role model by following through with the routines of the household.
- It's often easier to "see" the negative, so focus on all their good behaviors.
- Compliment your child if they act in an appropriate way when a peaceful transition was made with a quick acknowledgment and positive feedback.
- Babies are usually ready to begin a bedtime routine around two months old. Starting them early will assist in establishing good sleeping habits.
- Try to keep consistent nap, bedtime, and waking schedules.
- Stick to three meals and two snacks a day, at regular intervals, with no other food offered outside of those times.
- Set an allotted time for TV viewing each day and stick to it.
- Once a routine is established, try to organize your day around your child's, as consistent naps and bedtime are very important.

NAP AND BED TIME ROUTINES

Sleep is a very important aspect of your child's growth and development. Just as food fuels the body for growth, sleep also contributes to physical and mental development, as human growth hormone is released when a child sleeps. A lack of sleep often leaves kids feeling cranky and irritable, which ultimately means you'll be feeling the same way too!

Having the proper amount of rest each day will ensure children are alert and ready to play and learn. It also helps to keep them in a good mood, which benefits everyone. Regulating naps and nighttime sleeping patterns aids in a smooth transition from a busy day to a comfy bed. The use of a routine can make sleep time a fun part of the day, rather than a chore to be dreaded.

Naps

- Naps are best done in the comfort of a child's bedroom, or another consistent location.

- Carry out a small routine for naps, such as a story first, to ease the transition.

- Don't schedule a toddler tumbling class or other enrichment class at your child's naptime. Fortunately, most activities geared toward children have hours to suit every schedule.

- Remain flexible to the changes in your children as they get older. Naptimes can change every few months or so until they reach their final once-a-day nap in the afternoon, until none at all. Enjoy these hours of respite in your day…they don't last forever!

- Maintain a "quiet time" even when an older child no longer naps. It will give you a brief reprieve, and will help the child learn to entertain themselves.

Bed Time

Develop a solid and consistent bedtime routine, between thirty to sixty minutes, and stick to it as best as possible. Try to carry out the routine in a relaxed and calm environment in order to help your children settle down for the night.

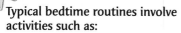

Typical bedtime routines involve activities such as:
- ➡ a bath
- ➡ brushing teeth
- ➡ reading books
- ➡ singing songs
- ➡ listening to quiet music
- ➡ a ritual such as a prayer or saying something you're thankful for that day
- ➡ saying goodnight to everyone, including pets and favorite toys
- ➡ cuddling, along with hugs and kisses
- ➡ "tucking in" teddy bears and dolls

- If possible, have both parents participate in the bedtime routine, either together or on alternate nights. This allows both spouses to experience this special time with their children, and makes children more comfortable if one parent is not available.

- Keep the same routine after dinner, so they know bedtime is coming.

- At bedtime have your child identify one thing they liked about the day. This helps to connect with each other and summarize the day.

- Resist lying down with your child to get them to sleep. This can be a very hard habit to break.

TRANSITIONS

Tips to Help You Along!

- Kids don't have a sense of time, so you need to establish sensible cues to help them. Try leading them into the next activity with prompts such as "When I'm done singing this song…", "When this show ends…".

- Give verbal time warnings ahead of time so the change does not come as a surprise. Stick by them for consistency.

- Use the same words each time, such as "clean up", "pick up" or "put away," instead of using them all interchangeably to help decrease confusion.

- Let children see something concrete. For example, say, "When the big hand is at the top of the clock, it's time to clean up".

- Use a timer to help indicate a change in activities.

- Sing a clean up song.

- Give your child age-appropriate choices. For example, when going outside let your child choose from two pairs of shoes. If it's time to clean up, let them decide what to put away first, or where to put things.

- Try taking pictures of buildings, people, and daily activities. Give them to your child when you are preparing to experience the photo's contents. This visual cue helps prepare a young child with poor language understanding.

Bath Time

Most children love to splash in the bath! While a lot of fun for the little ones, it can be a messy and arduous task for mom. However, accepting that floors will get wet, and that you probably will too, may help you to just relax and enjoy this pleasurable time with your kids. Making it a fun and non-stressful event will create a nice, happy wind-down to your child's day.

TIPS FOR BABIES

- Not all babies enjoy being bathed. They don't need to have a bath every day.
- With new infants, try a sponge bear to lay baby on – it's very comfortable and you can bathe them anywhere.
- Choose a bathtub for baby that has a reclining comfortable seat. You can lay a towel in the bottom to make it softer.
- Starting around 4-6 months, an inflatable bathing tub works great. It sits right in the tub and suctions to the wall when not in use. It is also portable for trips away from home.
- Johnson & Johnson's Head to Toe body wash is excellent – it can work as your bubbles, body wash, and shampoo.

TIPS FOR TODDLERS

- When toddlers want to start washing themselves, try the non-slip soap that's wrapped in mesh to make it easier.
- Use an empty ketchup bottle filled with water to rinse kids' hair so the water doesn't pour everywhere and get in their eyes.

- Buy the "snake" showerhead that can be lowered to a height that's perfect to rinse the hair and soapy bodies – they love taking "showers".
- If time allows, bathe kids separately, as it gives each child some individual splash time and eliminates opportunity for squabbles.
- During a bath, periodically close the shower curtain or shower door and let them have a "splash time," so water remains in the tub.
- Don't worry about the bathroom getting wet…it's only water, and it will dry!

BATH TOYS

- Children love simple, everyday items, such as Tupperware containers, funnels, plastic scoops and spoons or toy watering cans.
- Clean bath toys with bleach every once in a while, especially the squirt toys, as mold often builds up inside of them.

Put a stainless steel or plastic dish rack in the tub to hold and dry toys after a bath.

The "Witching" Hours

New mothers will find that late afternoon until children's bedtime will be the most challenging hours of the day. These hours are often packed with routines (meal, bath, and bed) at a time when children are either tired or wired. Throw in an exhausted parent and you have a potential brew of exasperation. To avoid ending every day at the end of your rope, do what you can to make this time period run as smoothly as possible.

BEWITCHING TIPS TO TRY

- Drop everything! Know that this is a tough time and prepare – don't take phone calls, plan to be at home, try to plan ahead.

- Have as much meal planning and preparation done in advance as possible. Make supper whenever you get time during the day, and heat it up as needed at meal time. Crock pots are ideal.

- If you are making dinner, allow the kids to "help" if possible. Giving them small things to do both keeps them busy and may entice them to eat what "they've" made.

- Stick to a schedule, and try to get everyone fed early.

- Get the children outside playing if possible – go for a walk, let them run around.

- Take walks in the stroller every afternoon.

- Carry baby in a sling, front pack, or backpack as they love the motion and it keeps them content.

- Save a special video or a favorite taped TV show that they are allowed to watch only at this time.

- Keep noise and extra stimulation to a minimum by turning off electronics.

- Play soothing music.

- Provide quiet activities, such as puzzles, coloring and story time.

- Have a "grab bag" of activities that only comes out during this time, so the activities will be more exciting.

- Provide a small, nutritious snack in mid-afternoon so that your children are not running out of fuel.

- Give yourself slack – if the kitchen's a mess, the playroom's a disaster, and you've given them noodles three nights in a row, don't worry, there's always tomorrow!

- Sing a lot of silly songs with actions, pillow fights, crazy dancing to music – anything to make your child laugh and be active so that they are ready for bed with happy thoughts.

- Loosen your grip on getting tasks done and spend time with the kids. Things will get done.

- Take cool-off time if you think you're going to lose it! Have one small area of your house that is always clean and organized, and take a five minute breather there to get yourself together (even if it's the bathroom!).

- When old enough, give the kids jobs to do such as setting the table, putting recyclables into bin, and cleaning up the toys.

Some of what makes this so tough is that we are trying to do everything! With patience waning and fatigue increasing, it is the worst time to tackle the chores that await us. Establish a routine that works for everyone.

"Some important gifts to give your children are love, comfort, safety, praise, and positive discipline."

5 . MEALS
Starting Baby on Solids

A major milestone has been reached when the time comes to introduce solid foods to your child. Your "little baby" suddenly seems so big now! This transition can be a very fun – and messy – experience. Be sure to keep a camera on hand for the many "Kodak moments" that will arise: facial expressions reacting to various tastes, messy hands and faces, food and bowls on heads! Enjoying this time as much as your baby does will make it a pleasant experience for both of you. Remember that you should only start feeding your child solids under the advice and guidance of your pediatrician!

WHEN IS BABY READY?

- At least four months old.
- Able to sit with support.
- Is reaching and grabbing.
- Seems unsatisfied after a feeding, or has shorter intervals between feedings.
- Shows interest by watching you eat, following your fork from plate to mouth, reaching for food on your plate, and mimicking eating behaviors.
- Eagerly opens mouth when sees spoon approaching.
- If child turns away at your attempts to feed, then they are not ready.

GETTING STARTED

- Initially, solids should be an addition to, not a substitute for, breastmilk or formula.
- When starting on solid food for the first few times, give a little milk or formula first to get the "edge" off hunger so they'll be more patient with the solids.

CEREAL

- Rice cereal is perfect to start with because it is easily digestible, followed by oatmeal and then barley. (Don't try mixed cereal until you have tried the individual grains first to see if there is an allergic reaction.)

FRUITS AND VEGETABLES

- Following cereal, fruits are easier to start with than vegetables, as they are sweeter and more appetizing. Babies are born with a "sweet tooth"– they have more sweet taste buds than any other. (The foremilk of breastmilk contains sugar, in order to entice the baby to drink.)
- Great starter fruits include applesauce, pears, and mashed bananas, which are all sweet-tasting and easily digestible.
- Great starter vegetables include sweet potatoes, winter squash, and carrots, which have good flavor and texture.
- Introduce one food at a time and wait five to seven days before starting the next one, so you can tell if they have an allergic reaction to it.

POSSIBLE SIGNS OF A FOOD ALLERGY:

- Bloating, gas or an upset stomach.
- Irritability.
- Congested or runny nose.
- Itchy skin or watery eyes.
- Sandpaper-like rash on face.
- Red rash around anus.
- Diarrhea or mucous in stool.
- Vomiting.

HELPFUL HINTS

- Use a baby spoon that turns white if a food is too hot to serve.
- Babies may take up to ten tries of a new food before they'll eat it.
- If you're having trouble starting a new vegetable or other food (after having been successful with a fruit), then try mixing applesauce in with it. Gradually decrease the amount of fruit you add.
- Let baby hold onto a small toy (such as a linking ring) or plastic spoon while you're feeding them, so they don't put their hands in their food, mouth, or hair.
- Use a hand-held food grinder or a mini food processor to puree your own fruits and vegetables, and cooked food – it's fresh, and also cost-effective. Adding a little water to the food will help you to achieve the desired consistency. Put pureed food into ice cube trays in the freezer (you can also buy special containers with lids for freezing). Once frozen, pop them out and store in freezer baggies. Just grab them and heat in microwave when it's mealtime. Prepare one month's food at a time, and you're all set.
- If your child does not like the uneven consistency of homemade baby food, then use organic jarred food. Even when they start eating "real" food, you can still supplement their nutrition with this food, especially the baby cereal, which has lots of iron in it.
- Keep jars of baby food on hand for ease when out and about, or traveling.
- Tiny pastas such as orzo or pastene, with butter, are good ones to start with after the fruits and vegetables.
- When you're upgrading from baby cereals to real cereals, choose healthy ones and let them get soggy in formula/ breastmilk first so it's easier to chew and swallow.

- Do not home-prepare beets, turnips, carrots or spinach for a baby under one year old. These vegetables contain large amounts of nitrates, which can cause anemia. Use commercial jars of baby food for these items, as baby food companies screen vegetables for this chemical.

Offer "new" foods in the morning, so that if it doesn't agree with the baby, any intestinal upset should be gone by bedtime.

WHEN IS BABY READY FOR FINGER FOODS?

- Interested in small objects.
- Uses a "pincer grasp" – picks up objects with thumb and forefinger.
- Wants to "do things myself".

GOOD FINGER FOOD STARTERS

- O-shaped cereal.
- Cooked pasta pieces.
- Toast.
- Baby cookies, graham crackers, teething biscuits.
- Rice cake pieces.
- Soft fruit pieces: bananas, canned peaches and pears.
- Small cooked vegetable pieces: carrots, potatoes, peas.
- Grated cheese and apples.

Keeping baby busy with finger foods on the highchair tray will give you a little extra time while preparing the dinner or cleaning up afterwards!

FOODS TO AVOID DURING THE FIRST YEAR

- **Potential allergy-causing foods** – over 90% of food allergies in young children are caused by: dairy products, soy, shellfish, wheat, tree nuts, peanuts, egg whites, citrus fruits, food additives.

- **Sugary foods** – if you avoid them when they're younger, your children will be less likely to desire them later on.

- **Salty foods** – too much sodium can be damaging to the kidneys. There is no innate preference for a salty taste, so avoid both adding it to food or foods that are high in it.

- **Cow's and goat's milk** – they don't provide the right proportion of nutrients for babies. After age one, start slowly with whole cow's milk. If a milk allergy is detected, ask your pediatrician about alternatives, such as rice or soy milk.

- **Honey and corn syrup** – can contain spores that cause botulism poisoning in babies.

- **Too much juice** – children should not drink more than 6-12 oz. per day, as it does not have the protein, fat and vitamins that breastmilk and formula contain. If you do serve juice, dilute it with water and serve in a sippy cup, not a bottle.

CHOKING HAZARDS

Raw vegetables
Whole grapes
Cherries
Raw apples and pears
Berries
Oranges or grapefruit
Raisins
Hot dogs
Nuts
Popcorn
Hard candy

Always monitor how much food your baby is putting in their mouth – even "soft" foods can be a choking hazard if there's too much in the mouth.

More Lifesavers

Meal Time

Three times a day, seven days a week – there's no avoiding meals! With children, it's important to be thinking about what and how much they consume. Starting them early with good eating habits helps to build a foundation for life-long healthy eating practices. While it is a huge responsibility to feed children healthily, it doesn't have to be an intimidating undertaking. These tried-and-true tips should help.

MEAL PLANNING

- Don't try to be Julia Child during the week – concentrate on easy, healthy meals. Pull out all the stops on the weekends when you may have extra helping hands.

- Try shopping at a health food store to discover a wider range of healthier choices.

- Think ahead when you're cooking – for example, double recipes to freeze, when making potatoes, make extras to save for the next day to mash and add tuna or salmon for fishcakes.

- Highlight good recipes in recipe books with sticky tabs that are labeled with the title, so that you can easily find what you're looking for without a lot of searching.

- Read the back of soup cans, pasta packages, and boxes of stuffing or rice for recipes that are usually very good, quick, and easy.

- Trade "tried and true" recipes with friends.

- Avoid offering a "menu" for kids – if they're hungry, they will eat what you serve!

Think ahead and plan four dinners a week. The other days can be leftovers or simple meals like eggs and toast, or pizza.

MEAL PREPARATION

- Buy meat in large packs, separate it into baggies, add marinade, and freeze it. When mealtime comes you just have to pull it out of the freezer and the right amount of meat is ready to go.

- Keep staples on hand for times when you need a quick meal that you haven't planned for. Good suggestions are pancake mix that you just add water, eggs and bread, frozen fruit, and healthy frozen foods.

- Buy ready-baked chickens in the grocery store and keep in the fridge to use for things such as sandwiches, salads and chicken quesadillas.

- Keep a shopping list handy and immediately write down ingredients you run out of.

- Freeze healthy muffins that you can pull out quickly for a snack, breakfast, dessert, or unexpected company.

- Take recipes for cookies and muffins that are "healthy" and add a few chocolate chips or raisins to make them more appealing to kids.

- When making muffins, use a non-stick spray instead of papers so that kids don't get frustrated pulling off the papers.

- Use a pizza cutter to cut through finger foods in a flash.

HINTS FOR KIDS

- Develop good eating habits in your children by modeling healthy eating behaviors yourself, including eating breakfast, healthy snacks, and vegetables on a consistent and regular basis.

- Offer a variety of choices to your children from early on so they learn to like many foods.

- Introduce new foods regularly, and insist children at least try everything on their plates. If they truly don't like something, they can set it aside after they've tasted it.

- As children get older, make them more of a part of choosing, preparing, and cleaning up the meals. They may show more interest in eating a wider variety of food if they are a part of the process.

- Most children love wearing little aprons when they're helping, and it helps to keep clothes clean too!

- If you have a picky-eater, try to put at least one thing on their plate you know they will eat, so the entire meal does not become a battle of wills.

- If your children don't seem to be hungry at mealtime, then limit snacks.

- Don't let your kids graze: offer snacks at snack time, and meals at mealtime.

- Let your kids "spread" things like butter and peanut butter on toast, or cream cheese on a bagel, with a plastic knife.

- Beginning at an early age, get children to carry their dishes (plastic plates, please) from table to sink, and even stack in the dishwasher with assistance. These good habits are much easier to start when they're novel and the kids are young.

TIME TO DINE

- Try to eat as a family at the table, as often as possible.

- Feed an infant first, and then let them sit near the table.

- Put a towel or mat under highchair/chair for easy clean-up of messy eaters.

- "Euro Chairs" work great for toddlers, as they are height-adjustable and keep children's feet on a solid surface.

- Serve meals at roughly the same time every night so kids become adjusted to being hungry at that time.

- Have everything at the table, including drinks, before you start the meal to avoid the disruption of getting up and down.

- Put everybody's plates on the table at the same time, otherwise the kids will finish before parents, and then you don't get the family time.

- Don't call kids to the table until the food is at the proper temperature to eat.

- Start each meal on a good note with a ritual, be it a prayer or what each person was thankful for during the day – it will set a calmer tone for the meal.

- Teach your kids good table manners EARLY.

- During meals, converse with your children about what they're eating, what they did that day, and plans for tomorrow.

- Deter messiness by having your kids participate in cleaning up the food that is on the floor after a meal.

- Eliminate watching TV or answering the phone during mealtimes – it should be family time.

THINK HEALTHY SNACKS

Snacks are an important part of your children's eating habits. Like stoking a fire, they provide the ongoing fuel needed for energetic children throughout the day. Try offering snacks two times a day, both mid-morning and mid-afternoon. By keeping them healthy and nutritious, you can take advantage of these occasions to "fill-in" areas of your children's diet that may be lacking. For example, if they don't drink milk with their meals, then offer cheese or yogurt as a snack; if they don't like eating meat, then try peanut butter on a small bagel. By focusing on healthy foods, you are setting your children down the path of lifelong good eating habits.

Easiest Muffin Recipe Ever

Here is a muffin recipe that is healthy and easy for kids to help with.

Simply mix one can of pumpkin with one box cake mix, such as carrot cake. Add raisins, walnuts, or chocolate chips if you wish. Pour batter into muffin tins. Bake at 350 degrees for 15-20 minutes.

Easy to whip up for unexpected guests, or freeze them for quick snacks.

IDEAS

- High-fiber cookies.
- Homemade trail mix. Include dried fruit, mini M&M's, peanuts, Cheerios, Life cereal, and pretzel sticks broken in half.
- Fruit and more fruit!
- "Bugs on a log" – celery or cucumber wedges with peanut butter or cream cheese, with raisins placed on top.
- Healthy muffins.
- String cheeses.
- Pretzels, popcorn, graham crackers, rice cakes.
- Peanut butter and jelly or banana on whole wheat bread.
- Apple slices with peanut butter dip.
- Yogurt.
- Freeze chunks of watermelon on a stick for healthy and tasty popsicles.
- Roll bananas in crushed pretzels.
- Freeze gogurts (yogurt in a tube).
- Frozen soybeans out of the pod (organic food section) – boil, and add salt.
- Pumpkin has a lot of vitamins, try using it in your baking.
- Soymilk fiber fruit smoothies blending vanilla soymilk, 1/2 banana, 4 frozen strawberries, 1/4 cup frozen peas and carrots and 1 tbsp. wheat germ.
- Toast wheat germ to use as sprinkles.
- Partially boil carrot sticks.
- Put snack-food into small baggies or small snack cups and keep in cupboard so you can grab them quickly.

A NOTE ON TODDLERS!

Feeding toddlers can be a very challenging task. Continuously changing appetites and a growing need for independence and control often butt heads at the kitchen table. A food loved one week moves to the bottom of the list the next. They'll refuse to eat for several days and then suddenly become a bottom-less pit. Sandwiches better be cut the RIGHT way, or a tantrum will ensue. Serving vegetables? Better muck getting them to eat dirt and worms. And the list goes on!

Just So You Know…

- It is normal for toddlers to refuse previously preferred foods or to refuse to try new foods altogether. Sometimes they need 20-30 exposures to a new food before they will eat it. Choose a new food, put small amounts on your child's plate at each meal and do not comment on it or draw attention to it. Most toddlers will immediately refuse a food if you push it on them.

- If you're having a hard time getting your toddler to eat a balanced diet, monitor what they eat over 5-7 days, not on a daily basis. If they eat a variety in that longer period of time, don't worry.

- Give them the "illusion of control" by offering two choices for a meal (both of which you are happy to prepare) and letting them choose what they would like.

Hints to Help with Vegetables

- Make edible veggie art pictures.
- Put different cut-up fruits or vegetables in an ice-cube tray or small muffin pan.
- Fill an ice-cream cone with cottage cheese and shredded veggies.
- Slip them into foods your child likes, such as cottage or cream cheese, and rice. Cover them with healthy sauces, such as tomato or cheese.
- Serve them with a dip. (kids love dip!)
- Cut them into interesting shapes.

Pretzels

You need:

1 pkg. yeast	1 tbsp sugar
1 1/2 cups warm water	4 cups flour
1 tsp. salt	1 egg, beaten

What to do:

1. Dissolve yeast in water.
2. Add salt, sugar, flour.
3. Stir mixture and knead until dough is smooth.
4. Roll dough and twist into letters, numbers or animals.
5. Lay on greased cookie sheet, brush with beaten egg, and sprinkle with salt.
6. Bake at 425 degrees for 12-15 minutes.

Note: *You can add food coloring to the mixture to create different colors.*

More Lifesavers

"Treat your children as you hope
they will one day treat theirs."

6 . FAMILY

Introducing a New Sibling

When a new sibling arrives, older children may initially experience some feelings of anxiety, frustration, and feeling left out when a new baby is brought home. After all, they will suddenly find they are no longer the center of the universe! Have no fear! These feelings are often short-lived when the child sees that a wonderful and precious addition has been made to the family. You can facilitate a smooth introduction of the new baby with some of these helpful suggestions.

SETTING THE STAGE

- Bring older siblings to prenatal appointments if possible.
- See if the hospital offers a class or workshop for siblings.
- Buy the older sibling a doll that they can pretend to take care of. Let them wash it, put on little diapers and pretend to feed it with a real bottle. When the baby comes, they can continue to take care of their little 'baby' while you take care of the 'real' one.
- Find a book or video relevant to a new sibling. A great video to try is Sesame Street's "Baby Bear and the New Baby".
- Talk to the older children and help them to realize what a special gift they are going to receive and love. Make sure they know deep in their hearts how special and unique they are, and the many ways a new member of the family will enhance all.
- Have older siblings help prepare for baby's arrival by painting something in the nursery, selecting baby clothes and toys, helping pick out names or planning a coming home birthday party.

- Close to the birth of the new baby, have a "big sister/brother" party.
- Try to have the older child socialize with a smaller baby, to get used to how fragile they are, and how to touch them gently.
- Prepare the sibling(s) beforehand regarding how much time will be spent with the baby, all about the nursing process and how tired mommy will be.
- Take the older children to a toy store to choose a gift for the new baby, and a small one for themselves as well. When the baby arrives, have the children give the baby their gifts, and allow them to open theirs.
- Remember to encourage family members to include siblings if bringing a gift for the baby.

Don't panic when toddlers desire to be affectionate with the baby, as their innocent devotion is measurably more important than any germ contact. Monitor their actions to ensure no unintentional or intentional overly physical contact. Teach them how to respect physical boundaries, and then let them love each other!

THE ARRIVAL

- Have dad bring the older sibling to hospital to see MOM when no one else is visiting. Have baby in the nursery, and after the visit get baby and introduce them.
- Have a "surprise" bag of goodies for older siblings at the hospital.
- Have mom enter the house by herself to greet the older siblings. Allow special time for older ones to do something "fun."
- Give older children a sense of responsibility by enrolling them in the care of the baby as they are able, with tasks such as feeding, bathing, walking, getting diapers and putting things away.
- Let the sibling hold the new baby with assistance, giving them lots of praise and attention.
- Have someone else spend a few hours with the baby so you can spend good, quality time with the older child.
- Parents should continue to do special things alone with their older children to be sure they know they are loved and valued.
- Be in tune with their feelings, and deal with any issues as they arise.

- Keep siblings in regular routines, and continue the same discipline for disobedience, not just what makes it easier for you at the moment.
- Let the sibling share in all the "firsts." Express how the baby is "OURS" as a family.
- It is not unusual for older children to regress a bit in their skills for a couple of months after the birth of a sibling.
- Prepare a basket of special activities for older children, and reserve it for when you are nursing or bottle feeding.

Despite all of your preparations, be prepared that your child WILL likely be jealous and angry, but it's good for them to learn they are not the center of the universe – they will get over these negative emotions and will be happy to have a playmate. During the beginning of the transition they need LOTS of reassurance and affirmation, and it's a good opportunity to empathize and help label their feelings. They need acceptance, clarity of boundaries, and tons of hugs and kisses!

More Lifesavers

New Experiences

While most adults get a little anxious before a new experience, these feelings are often magnified in the minds of youngsters. Imaginations can go wild at the thought of a visit to the doctor or dentist, or the first day of preschool. Parents have the challenge of merging children's perceptions with realistic expectations of a new or uncomfortable experience. These ideas should help to get you started!

PREPARATION IS KEY

- Read a book about the experience. A great resource is the First Experience Books (set of 6) by Usborne Books, with topics including: going to the hospital, dentist, doctor, school, the new puppy, and going on a plane. The "Little Critter" books, by Mercer Mayer also have many good preparation stories.

- Get recommendations about dentists, pediatricians and hair salons.

- Act out a doctor's visit, using a doctor's kit. If your child is anxious about getting shots, role playing will really help, along with explaining WHY they get vaccinations.

- Reassure them that a doctor or dentist visit is for their well-being. Let them know what to expect, that it's necessary, and that big people do it too.

- Talk about the activity several days in advance to get them used to hearing about it.

- Always tell them the truth about the pending experience, and remember that the less build-up the better!

- Visit the place ahead of time and answer any questions that are asked, since giving too much information can be overwhelming.

- Introduce a positive model, such as someone else giving a testimony about their experience, or talk about their friends who have had a similar experience.

- Be a good role model. Talk about your own similar experiences.

- Keep your own discomfort from showing, as children will pick up on your vibes. If you have issues with the dentist, for example, perhaps your spouse can take your child to the appointment.

- Offer them a treat for handling the experience well.

Kids seem to pick up on all our adult fears, so as a parent you must put on a happy face whenever possible, as it makes for a long walk when your child is afraid of a fly!

More Lifesavers

Adjusting to a Move

Moving to a new home can be a very stressful experience for a toddler or preschooler. It is a major disruption of the daily foundation they've become adjusted to. Adequately preparing your children for the event is the first step in ensuring a successful transition.

BEFORE THE MOVE

- Show children a map of the country or local area to illustrate where they live now and where they're going.

- Take a picture of the new house and visit it if possible before moving.

- Enlist children's "help" with the packing. Let them make the boxes by cutting tape, have them draw on the boxes with crayons, put stickers on them, crinkle the packing paper to put inside. Don't forget that they can amuse themselves for hours just playing with the empty boxes!

- Keep their rooms as normal as possible for as long as possible before you move by packing up their rooms last.

- If possible, have a cleaning service clean the new house before your belongings arrive, so you're not overwhelmed with both cleaning and unpacking.

- While the moving truck is being packed up, keep your children safely out of the way and occupied by finding a friend or family member to watch them.

- Make sure children have their personal, familiar items with them at all times during the move.

- Have a going away party at the old home with children's friends and neighbors – give them all note cards and envelopes stamped and addressed to your children at the new home.

DURING THE MOVE

- Arouse excitement about their new room – make it feel like a fun adventure!

- Keep your children out of the house during the move, then return them to the new house with the bedrooms all set up with familiar toys and blankets.

- Try to put your children's things in the same approximate locations they were in the old house.

- At the new location, try to stay in a hotel with a pool or fun diversions throughout the move. Parents can take turns watching the kids at the hotel (keeping them out of the way) and unpacking.

- Display pictures of child with family members who no longer live close by.

Allow children to pick their new bedrooms if possible. Set up their new rooms first, even if nothing else gets done that day.

AFTER THE MOVE

- Get back into routines as quickly as possible.

- Explore new territory together as a family. Make it a priority to learn what the fun things are to do in your new town, such as parks, attractions, walks and restaurants.

- Go for lots of walks and introduce yourself to neighbors, hopefully getting the scoop on the neighborhood and meeting families with kids.

- Introduce the process of writing and mailing letters.

Quality Fun Time

Often our lives get so hectic and scheduled that we forget about just spending time together as a family. Special family time is very valuable to children, regardless if it's a quiet activity at home, or out on a fun adventure. Setting aside time that is "just for them" lets them know how special and important they are. These are the times your children will remember, so get out and have fun!

FUN FAMILY TIME

- Maintain connections with family and friends by establishing rituals such as Friday pizza and game night, Saturday morning breakfast, or a Sunday afternoon cookout.
- Use the great outdoors – hikes, beach, bike riding, walks, picnics, boating, sledding, and skating.
- Setting "family time" aside is important. You don't have to make elaborate plans – just going for a walk near your home or picking up an ice cream.
- Have regular "special time" once a week where each child chooses an activity to do one on one with the parent of their choice.
- Pack a picnic and find a scenic spot near the water where there's lots of space to run, walk, and kick a ball around.
- Have a family movie night.
- Go to a family theater in your local community.
- Split up during family activities if the children are at different developmental stages so that everyone has a good time.
- Seasonal activities such as apple picking, winter carnivals, sleigh rides, ice skating, and building sand castles.
- Camping – even if it's in the backyard; bonfires at appropriate age.
- For a mini vacation from it all, drive to a campground mid-afternoon and select a campsite to build a fire. Roast hot dogs for dinner and marshmallows for dessert; put everyone back in the car to sleep at home!
- Singing and dancing.
- Gardening activities – let them plant and take care of their own flowerbed or vegetable garden.

- Make a walk into a "mystery hunt" (search for signs of spring, or count Christmas trees, or count animals); stop and guess what others hear or see.
- Swimming classes and free swims, join a summer swim club.
- Children's museum, aquarium, nature center, and zoo.
- Organized activities: Kindermusik, Gymboree, open gyms at local gymnastic facilities, Y programs, and local Parks and Recreation programs.
- Special "cuddling" routines before bed are special, reading favorite books and chatting about the activities of the day.

If you do things together as a family, then many activities will be memorable regardless of what they are. It's the TIME spent together, not necessarily WHAT is done.

NEED MORE IDEAS?

- Libraries often have free museum passes available and lists of local venues to visit.
- Local parent magazines.
- "Weekend" section of newspaper.

At Christmas time, make a paper chain and starting on December 1st take off a "link". Each link has an activity (donate some needed items to a shelter, give away old toys, write letters to Santa, or have a pizza party under the Christmas tree). It's a fun count-down to Christmas and a great way to bond with your family.

Memories

There is nothing more sacred than the precious memories of all the journeys your children will take on the road to adulthood. Preserving them for present and future enjoyment is a wonderful and invaluable gift to yourself and your family.

PRESERVING SPECIAL MEMORIES

- Make a time capsule for your child of the "day you were born" – include things such as newspaper (either whole or cut out with stories, weather, flyer with cost of food and toys), postage stamps, coins of the year, photo of child and parents in hospital.
- Frame hand and footprints on matte paper, labeled with name and date.
- Keep your children's favorite blankets, clothing items, and shirts from sports teams they played on, and use these materials to create a memory quilt for each child as they leave for college, or have someone make it for you.
- Keep 'special' kids' clothing items in a cedar chest to pass along to THEIR children.
- Every birthday, put a photo of your child in a large frame and have family and friends sign the matting with special messages and colorful stickers.
- Write a letter to your child every year on their birthday and seal it in an envelope. Include your observations, milestones your child has achieved, accomplishments and wishes for your child. Present the envelopes to them when they are older.

JOURNALS

- Write things down! You probably will regret it later if you don't mark your children's milestone, quirks, and funny things they have said or done. JOURNALS ARE IRREPLACABLE and can be done in a few stolen minutes every few days.
- Allow other family members, friends and babysitter to participate in entering thoughts in a journal.
- Ask parents and grandparents to write down memories of family, in order to pass along precious family history.

- If you feel like you don't have enough time to write in a journal, then you can:
  - ➡ Use a regular wall calendar to jot down children's milestones and fun things you did. Keep it in a convenient location for easy access; store all of the calendars in a plastic container, and twenty years later you'll have years of memories at your fingertips and will have spent very little time doing it.
  - ➡ On the last day of every month write things down in a journal that occurred that month, as you'll be more likely to stick with it if it's only once in a while and it's on a routine basis.
  - ➡ Write an entry each birthday preserving special and unique qualities and memories of your child particular to that year.
  - ➡ Use a "1st Year Calendar" that marks milestones.

Keep a family journal on the table each day. You can express your feelings for the events of the day, things children said, activities your family has done. Keep the journal open for reading by all members of the family. They can write their own feelings and comments in the journal as well. As the children get older and the days get busier, you can express your own pride, love and frustrations in the book and your children can do the same. If there's an argument where neither side feels heard by the other, it can be the place where, at calmer moments, each party can write their feelings and the dialogue continues on paper. Young children can share by drawing a picture and dictating to you what it might be. When your children get older, it's a place you can tell them you love them without embarrassing them, and it's a place for you to write your concerns. You will gather a beautiful collection of journals over the years!

MEMORY BOXES

- Have a memory box for each child where you save baby mementos, such as hospital ID bracelet, hand and footprints, lock of hair, baby socks, baptismal candle, naming document, cute things said and done, special art projects.
- Make a memory box out of souvenirs and photos from vacations or day trip spots; keep glass jars of sand, shells, and stones labeled with date and place.
- Photo boxes work great!
- Decorate your memory box with child's hand and footprints.

SCRAPBOOKS

- Scrapbooking is great, although keep it simple – grander scrapbooks are a lot harder to keep up with, and you might get discouraged and just stop doing it altogether.
- Try getting a small group of friends together who want to scrapbook, and meet monthly to work on a few pages at a time, and socialize!
- Scrapbook the first year of kids' lives in their own books, then make family albums after that.
- If you feel like you don't have time to keep a scrapbook, try doing it just for special occasions, such as the kids' birthdays and holidays.

PHOTOS

- Invest in a good photo printer and quality paper that doesn't allow photos to fade.
- Use a digital camera to keep photos organized by month on a disc. Download on your home computer and back up files regularly.

- If you take your film to get printed, as soon as you get them back put one set into a photo album and use the second set to give away, or let kids look at. This way you'll have them all in an album, instead of stacks of photos that you may get so behind on they end up being shoved in a box until you're a grandparent!
- Keep a special album for each child, with pictures of special moments, such as coming home from the hospital, sitting in high chair, crawling, walking, and their 1st birthday.
- Take digital photos of art projects and paintings so you have a record of the progression and development of skills, while saving only a few favorites.
- Use a camcorder for all special occasions as the children grow – be sure to get them talking, as nothing is cuter than the sound of their little voices!

GIFTS

- Family and friends will always treasure hand and footprints on something given as gifts, such as holiday ornaments, coffee mugs, photo frames or stepping stones.
- Share your children's art projects with people living far away – it keeps them feeling close to your children.
- Buy matted letters of your children's names, and insert photos of them for gifts or decorations.
- Awesome gift idea: a memory album that has calendars made up for the whole year, so the mother only has to fill in the information. Include pre-made pages for special events and milestones, such as first bath, holiday, meal, birthday, so that pictures just need to be added.

"Always talk to your child
from infancy on – they do understand
what you say!"

7. JUST FOR MOMS
Taking Care of Yourself

Taking time for you is essential for a healthy life and balanced parenting. Everyone, especially a busy mother, needs time to recharge their batteries. Not only does time away from the children provide a breath of fresh air, it also helps you to stay connected with the rest of the world. Women are notorious for not focusing on themselves once a child comes along. However, you will find yourself feeling re-energized once you GET OUT! So find the time and have some fun. Plan ahead and schedule time for yourself as often as possible.

FINDING THE TIME

- Find a babysitter either before or soon after your child is born, and use them on a regular basis so they get to know your child, and you are able to get a regular break.
- Plan for a sitter to come for a set time every week, or enlist a mother's helper. Even if you're at home, kids love playing with someone energetic.
- Do not be afraid to ask relatives to help for a couple of hours here and there.
- Get up early before the rest of your family to exercise or to have a cup of coffee in peace.
- Try to have children nap at the same time each day, so you can rest during that time. Have older children play by themselves or watch a movie.
- A schedule of going to bed early, for example by 7:30 pm, leaves the evening free to do what you want to do. You may have to get up a bit earlier in the morning, but everyone can use a little more morning time to get ready for the day!

Try a "snooze cruise" – take a car ride for the kids to fall asleep at nap time. Park somewhere with an appealing vista, listen to the radio, do a favorite hobby, read or lock the doors and take a nap yourself!

HAVE FUN!

- Plan a regular date night with your spouse. Take a long drive, go to dinner, see a movie and make the time to connect!
- Focus special attention on YOU. Enjoy a manicure and pedicure, massage, facial, or have your hair done.
- Go to the mall or a bookstore BY YOURSELF and shop FOR YOURSELF!
- Plan to go out with your girlfriends one night a month. Set the dates in advance and put them on your calendar so it really happens.
- Alternate sleeping in on Saturday mornings with your spouse.
- Seek out volunteer work.
- Pamper yourself with a candlelit bath with bubbles and your favorite "treat."
- Read a good book and join a book club.
- Work on a craft project or hobby.
- Go out by yourself for Saturday morning breakfast.
- Enjoy a ladies tea at a local teahouse.
- Start a business or project with another parent... you'll be amazed how fun it is.
- Drop in and paint pottery at a do-it-yourself location. Most places will let you bring your own munchies and favorite beverage.
- Join a gym with a friend and work out together while the kids play in the childcare room.
- Take a class at a local college which offers non-credit courses in subjects such as Yoga, conversational Italian or whatever else piques your interest. Never stop learning and stretching your boundaries!

Staying Connected

Socializing is imperative soon after your baby is born. The blues may sink in if you feel as though you have a limited existence once all the relatives and friends have gone home.

Both stay at home and working parents tend to feel like they are "out of the loop!" Never fear, having children can be one of the most social times of your life. Being open to new relationships outside of your existing circle of friends is crucial. If you are willing to forge new relationships, your life will be very fulfilled on those long, cold, winter days when you want to visit another person in the same situation.

We often ponder how meaningful our social lives have become since having kids... they have opened the door to new, wonderful, and fulfilling relationships!

GET YOURSELF OUT THERE!

- Take a birthing class, connect with someone who lives near you, and stay in touch.

- Find out about mother/baby groups at local hospitals or join organizations such as MOPS (mothers of preschoolers) and Mothers and More, an organization dedicated to improving the lives of mothers (www.mothersandmore.org).

- Shower and get dressed every day, so you FEEL like socializing.

- After doctor's approval, take baby shopping, out to friendly restaurants, and to other people's homes.

- Get outside! Walking is a great way to feel connected to the rest of the world.

- Go to the mall if you need to see some fresh faces. There's always a friendly face that will smile and compliment "your sweet baby."

- Maintain at least one interest outside of baby and resume the activity as soon as you are able to leave your baby.

- Participate in enjoyable activities with your child to meet other mothers, such as YWCA/YMCA Play and Swim programs, hospital sponsored playgroups, religious centers, baby yoga, Gymboree, open gyms and library hours.

- Walk around your neighborhood and scope out which homes have kids' toys and swing sets outside. Introduce yourself; you'd be surprised how many people are grateful to meet someone in their neighborhood who also has children.

Push yourself get out there, even if you're tired, shy, or nervous about taking the baby out. Just do it! Babies are more mobile than you may think.

BECOMING PART OF A PLAYGROUP

- Start a playgroup yourself! A group of 4 moms works out well, as it's inevitable that one of the moms will have to cancel but the group can maintain a rhythm and consistency. The goal is to be with other moms at least once a week.

- Find moms with similar parenting styles, including discipline and behavioral expectations.

- Keep it relaxed so you don't feel like you're entertaining.

- Rotate houses fairly; never burden ONE home and host.

- Learn to get past not always having a clean house. Your guests, especially other moms, just want to visit with you and your family.

When Spouses Travel

Parenting becomes even tougher when a spouse's job requirements involve traveling for extended periods of time. Suddenly you are left with the challenge of being "on" twenty-four hours a day. Without the welcomed breaks you get from a spouse, these times alone can be difficult and tiring. Planning and organization prior to their departure can help to make the days easier. Maintaining routines and activities will help to make the parent's absence less disruptive to family life. It is also important to try to keep the children connected to the absent parent. With sensitivity, consistency, and love, the time will pass by less stressfully.

HOW TO STAY CONNECTED

- Have pictures of the traveling parent around where the child can touch and hold them.
- Talk about the traveling parent often and schedule regular phone calls.
- Allow and encourage older children to write, email, and phone their traveling parent.

MAKING THINGS EASIER

- Before your spouse leaves, make sure you have the house stocked with food and other necessities.
- Remain consistent with discipline and routines.
- Make sure you tell friends and family that you'll be alone, and ask for help if needed. You will be pleasantly surprised with the offers you get!
- Schedule play dates, and time with family and friends.

- Plan an evening meal with another family or parent whose spouse is also traveling. This will fill the most difficult time of day and provide social opportunities.
- Do a kid-swap with you watching your friend's kids, and then having them watch yours so you can get some errands done.
- It's inevitable that a child may get sick or other unforeseen things happen. Have a good relationship with a neighbor or a friend close by to help in a time of need.
- Have all emergency phone numbers in a visible area.
- Schedule a babysitter in advance to help out during this time, so you can take a nap, or get some quiet time.
- Do what you need to do to make life less stressful for you. If your house gets messy, your kids don't get bathed, or you order a lot of take-out, it's OK!
- Enjoy quiet solitude when the kids are tucked in.
- Allow time for traveling parent to adjust back into the home.

More Lifesavers

_____

_____

_____

_____

_____

Balancing Work Life

Women who work outside the home have the dual challenge of juggling the pressures of a career along with the demands of children and a household. The key to success is keeping priorities straight and being organized.

STRATEGIES

- Establish a relationship with reliable and trustworthy childcare providers.
- Investigate the possibility of a job-share or flexible work schedule.
- Discuss and negotiate a solid work and childcare plan with your spouse. Each parent needs to have shared responsibility for a unified family structure.
- Use the leverage you have at the end of your maternity leave when your employer is desperate for you to come back, to push for a flexible schedule.
- Do your best to set boundaries regarding schedule and workload – it may not be reasonable for employers to expect that 60-hour week you put in prior to birth.
- Be upfront about any challenges with your employer. For example, if you're concerned about your ability to continue breastfeeding if faced with a business trip, be direct about your concern instead of mentioning another excuse for fear of embarrassment.

- Change how you use the workday. Think of strategies to become more efficient with your work and family life, such as working odd hours, or working longer days in exchange for a shorter workweek.
- Don't take on responsibility for everything at home. If possible, hire the necessary people to help with chores, such as a cleaning service or a grocery delivery service.
- Don't try to 'make up lost time' with the children by buying things for them and catering to every whim. It is best to remain consistent in discipline and habits.
- Don't be afraid to ask for help – no one can be "supermom".
- Prepare everything the night before by laying out clothing, have backpacks, bottles and food ready to go.
- Plan one day a week that you're going to cook, and freeze meals for the upcoming week and reheat when needed.

Prepare dinner ahead of time using a slow cooker.

More Lifesavers

_____

_____

_____

_____

_____

_____

When the Going Gets Rough

There is no doubt that motherhood is demanding. It can be a challenge to maintain your composure during the stressful times, be it a first time mother calming a crying infant, several small children demanding equal attention, or dealing with an irrational two year old. Couple this with the daily stressors of managing a household and inevitably reach a point when you feel a little "out of control." You are not alone with your feelings of frustration and helplessness!

Always remember that you are a teacher and role model to your children. How you conduct yourself in these stressful situations will play a large factor in how they behave when engaged in relationships of their own. Teach your children boundaries, values, morals, and respect by demonstrating them yourself. Chaotic situations can be controlled when you are armed with strategies to deal with your children in a positive manner. Keep yourself calm, cool, and collected by implementing some of the following tactics.

- Be gentle with yourself and listen to your heart.
- Phone a friend or family member.
- Phone a parenting hotline.
- Escape to an area of the house that is quiet for 5 minutes.
- Light a favorite scented candle.
- Play a favorite CD and listen with headphones.
- Have a stash of goodies to sweeten the moment, such as chocolate or caramels.
- If you have more than one child, prioritize and concentrate on one child's immediate needs at a time. Don't try to do three things at once!
- Take time for yourself by putting on your child's favorite video or DVD.
- Sing a song out loud (try Kum-by-ah!).
- Use positive "self-talk". Have some inspiring or calming phrases to say, such as, "this will pass", "they grow up too fast" or "they're only children and their brains are not fully developed".
- Put each child in the safety of their own rooms for 15 minutes.

- Read the funny little quips or a short story from Readers Digest.
- Phone your spouse at work and ask them to come home a little earlier, if possible.
- Seek out a sitter or mother's helper to see if they're immediately available to come over and play with the kids.
- Do some yoga or tai chi moves – perhaps the kids will join in! Relieve tension by taking deep, cleansing breaths along with gentle stretching.
- Join a meditation class for tips and ideas keep you centered.
- Keep pictures visible to keep yourself grounded and to remember your life in the "bigger picture" rather than the immediate moment.
- Remember a serene, peaceful place to comfort you. Visualize the place and the feelings it generates.

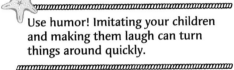

Use humor! Imitating your children and making them laugh can turn things around quickly.

Advice From the Trenches: Part Two

Our trusted contributors provided so many wonderful tips we were left with a hodge-podge of advice that was too valuable to leave out. So, wade through and see what you can use!

TRIED AND TRUE MOTHERING TIPS!

- If kids get "crusties" forming around nostrils when they have colds, clean with a q-tip and warm water, and then prevent the problem by applying Vaseline around the area.

- Take advantage of Early Intervention and preschool screenings to check your child's development.

- When a child starts preschool, have them get ready in the morning, before they engage in any activities around the house. This motivates the dawdlers and helps to ensure you'll leave the house on time.

- Keep a "Boo-Boo Bear" (terry cloth ice gel pack) in freezer for all the little bumps and bruises that occur.

- Using wireless 3 channel intercoms will help you to keep an ear on your children in other areas of the house, such as play rooms.

- Every once in a while, let kids have a pajama day – and you too!

- Nip your first child's behavioral issues in the bud, as a second child will very quickly model the older one's behavior.

- Try to set aside time everyday to give each child your full attention one-on-one. You can talk, play, read, or do an activity or game.

- Smile, even if you don't feel like it. It is contagious, and your children pick up on your moods and will be much happier if you are!

EXTRA! EXTRA! READ ALL ABOUT IT!

- Have your house completely child-proofed so that you don't always have to spend all of your time in the same room the child is in. You'll never get anything done otherwise!

- If you have the option to do a house-hold task now or later, DO IT NOW! Procrastinating will only add more stress later when all the little jobs build up. The only exception will be when you have a newborn. Do it later and sleep instead… let dad, grandma or a friend help you.

- Give yourself an extra 15 minutes (+5 minutes per additional child) for any time-sensitive tasks, such as leaving the house, doing a project or making meals. This allows for the unexpected – dirty diapers, potty, tantrums, spills, and the independent wills of youngsters! For example, if you need to leave the house by 8:45 am to get somewhere, plan to leave at 8:30 for one child, 8:25 for 2.

- Read the paper and listen to the news and weather on the TV or radio, to stay connected to the rest of the world.

- Don't over-schedule yourself! If you have enough time to spend at home enjoying your children, you'll save yourself some unnecessary stress.

- Keep an extra set of house and car keys hidden somewhere for those times when you are locked out.

- Keep some kind of "treat" such as coffeecake or muffins in the freezer that you can pull it out for unexpected guests.

- Keep a magazine you enjoy reading out on your kitchen counter so you can catch glimpses while you're preparing meals or waiting for microwaves.

- Always write things down! Put appointments, play dates, and other obligations on a calendar, and make a daily to-do list. Your memory may tend to diminish when you have a hundred things going on in your head! Keep your list and calendar open and available to see first thing each morning.

- Tape inspirational quotes, poems and pictures on the inside of your kitchen cabinets so you can read and appreciate them often.

- Use a black marker and white paper to label objects around the house to teach everyday words to your preschooler.

- Do a cookie swap with your friends during the holidays so you only have to bake one type of cookie (which is faster), while still yielding a nice variety.

- Buy automatic shut-off appliances so you don't have to worry about anything being left on.

- Birthday Express (www.birthdayexpress.com) has great "theme" items, toys, and costumes you can buy very cheaply, to use as rewards, dress-up costumes, or to pull out on a rainy day.

- Always keep super glue and various sized batteries on hand.

- Buy the same brand of sippy cup to decrease the confusion of different stoppers and lids.

Wear clogs! They slip on and off quickly and go with almost any outfit.

More Lifesavers

"Always find something good about the work children do – constant encourage-ment breeds high self-esteem and success."

Money Saving Ideas

Without a doubt, children are expensive! How quickly they outgrow clothes and shoes, not to mention growing interests in toys and activities. Day care, babysitting, pre-school, sports, hobbies, and lessons of all sorts – the expenses just keep building! Taking advantage of every opportunity to save money when you can will go a long way in stretching your budget, and still provide the things you want for your priceless children.

IN GENERAL

- Shop at wholesale stores, such as Sam's Club, BJ's, or Costco for bulk purchases.
- Create space in your house to store items that come on sale, or items you buy in bulk, such as diapers and wipes, toilet paper, Kleenex and detergent.
- Go in person or online and check out the clearance section of clothing and toy stores.
- Borrow things from friends, such as baby items and clothing.
- Collect coupons for baby food and formula and join online coupon clubs.
- Join baby clubs that send free samples, magazines, and coupons.
- Try using the more inexpensive diapers. They're often just as good.
- Take time to shop around and compare costs when purchasing more expensive items.
- Single-serve food items might be convenient when packing the diaper bag or lunch box, but filling a Tupperware or Ziploc baggie will be a lot cheaper in the long run.
- Plan a menu for the week, make a list and stick to it at the grocery store so you don't overspend when you get there, to avoid impulse buying.
- Buy seasonal items when you see them at the stores, so you're not overspending in desperation at convenience stores. Or better yet, cheaply buy seasonal items ahead for the following year at the end of the season when they're on clearance.
- Pay household bills immediately when you receive them to avoid late charges due to mail being "set aside" for later, and then forgotten about.

- Plan ahead when you see sales, and stock up when you can. You can save a lot of money by purchasing things such as birthday party supplies, baby supplies, and household goods ahead of time.

TOYS

- Shop at second-hand children's stores. You can get lots of great deals, especially on outdoor plastic items, such as tables, cars, small play gyms.
- If you find a sale on toys, buy a few things to store and keep on hand for birthday parties, rainy days or upcoming holidays.
- Put away toys that aren't being used frequently, and rotate them periodically. A toy that has been put away for a few months is BRAND NEW!
- Buy things at yard sales, although make sure toys are in good shape and safe for your child.
- Purchase toys that will grow with your child.
- Do a toy-swap with friends for 1-2 months at a time.

Don't spend money on a lot of fancy toys. It's better for them to use their imagination! Banging on pots and pans with wooden spoons is great fun, and empty boxes can become forts with couch pillows and a flashlight!

CLOTHING

- Purchase clothing at end-of-season sales for the following year. If you don't know what size your child will be, ask experienced friends. Leave the items in the store's bag with receipts, and pack away until the next year. Most stores (e.g. Baby Gap, Child's Place, and Gymboree) will take returns on items at any time as long as the tags are on and you have the receipt, but be sure to check the store's policy.

- Use clothing extenders for onesies.
- Shop at outlet stores.
- Buy children's clothing in larger sizes to extend their use.
- Second hand stores often have clothes with tags still on them for less.
- Set up your washer and dryer in a location that is convenient for you. If so, your children do not need a lot of clothes, as you will be able to throw in a load every few days.

More Lifesavers

Housecleaning

Undoubtedly the bane of your existence, trying to keep a clean and organized home is an admirable goal. As if taking care of small children isn't already a full-time job, you have an entire household seeking your attention on a daily basis. Messes accrue faster than a litter of bunnies – what's straightened up one minute is turned upside down the next! Hopefully some organizing and strategizing will help to make this daunting task feel a little more manageable.

KEEP IT SIMPLE!

- Establish a routine for cleaning the house, and stick to it.
- Keep a stock of basic cleaning supplies at all times, buying in bulk when possible.
- Clearly divide chores with spouse so there's won't be any misunderstandings over who's responsible for doing what.
- Confine toys to a designated play area in the house and let the area stay messy until kids are done playing for the day. Otherwise, it's a never-ending battle.
- Keep decorative baskets everywhere to catch items that tend to be left around the room or piled up on counters. Have one by the stairs to load toys and things that collect downstairs over the course of the day that need to go up and be put away. This decreases trips up and down, and helps keep things tidier.
- Have seasonal boxes on hand and labeled for easy storage and retrieval.

HOUSEKEEPING STRATEGIES

- Do a general straightening up on a daily basis, with one chore to complete daily, such as vacuuming and dusting.
- Take advantage of the 5-10 minute breaks you get here and there throughout the day to clean or straighten something. Waiting for a large chunk of time to do a whole cleaning job is probably not realistic.
- Choose one room of the house to clean each day, for example Monday the kitchen, Tuesday the bathrooms, Wednesday the playroom.

- Everyday, choose one household project. Whether it takes 20 minutes or 2 hours, as soon as it's done, you're done. Your tasks will seem less overwhelming if you focus on one at a time.
- De-clutter the house once a month. Keeping clutter to a minimum allows you to spend cleaning time cleaning, instead of sorting. Recycle or dispose of unwanted items often.
- Choose one spot in your home to display artwork, rotating pieces so that they don't get scattered throughout the house.
- Every spring, splurge and get assistance with the general cleaning of your house if you don't have the time to do a really thorough job yourself.
- Always use kid-friendly and pet-safe carpet cleaning agents, whether you're cleaning yourself or having someone do it for you.
- If at all possible, hire a cleaning service!

Don't go to bed with a dirty kitchen. It's a really tough way to start your next day!

QUICK CLEAN-UPS

- Accept that you probably won't have time to clean the house from top to bottom at one time, and make the most of a 30-minute cleaning spree.
- Have a dust buster and small broom and dustpan readily available for small messes.

- Keep a squirt bottle handy for spills to avoid having to mop the whole floor. Have a separate sponge or cloth by the sink for wiping up floor messes.

- As you are able, pick up things as you see them out of place instead of waiting for a colossal mess.

- Keep disinfectant cleaning wipes in the bathroom and every evening pull one out and to do a speedy wipe-down.

- Every day, try to spend 20 – 30 minutes on cleaning. This makes it more bearable and manageable.

- Wet and dry Swiffers clean up dirt and messes quickly and easily.

- The Mr. Clean magic eraser is great for easy removal of marks on walls.

- Wipe up food on tables, counters, floors, and appliances right away, as it takes a lot longer after the food dries up.

- Line cooking pans and dishes with a non-stick spray or non-stick aluminum foil when baking for fast and easy clean-up.

- A clean bathroom and a clean kitchen sink make the house appear clean, even if it's not!

If you're expecting visitors and don't have time to do a proper clean-up, take a laundry basket and gather all the clutter. Later, when you have time, go through the basket and put everything where it belongs. Bathtubs, shower stalls, and laundry rooms also make great spots to hide clutter in a hurry!

ENLIST YOUR CHILDREN

- Plant the seed early in your children's minds that it's their home, they are part of the family, and they are responsible for helping out. As soon as they are one year old, have them start helping to clean up, such as putting toys away or putting clothes into a hamper.

- Make clean-up prideful!

- Be a good role model with keeping your own space neat. Children will be more motivated to follow suit in keeping their own things tidy and organized.

- Have a routine with your children whereby they assist with simple chores on a regular basis.

- Put toy boxes in each room so toys are not dragged all over the house. Each child can be assigned one room to be cleaned up at the end of the day.

- Make cleaning a game to get a lot of participation without nagging. As children get older, put on a favorite CD, turn it up loud and agree that when the music is over the cleaning is done for the day.

- Use clear plastic bins with labels (picture labels for toddlers) so kids can see what's in them, to make sorting through messes easier.

- Children love the little housecleaning toys they can use to help with, such as brooms, vacuums, and dust busters.

LAUNDRY

- Try to locate the washer and dryer in a convenient, easily accessible location. Some dryers do not need to be vented to the outside.

- Apply stain remover immediately and soak once you remove your child's clothes.

- Clorox bleach pens work great for small stains on whites. White clothes are actually easy to keep clean!

- Find a chart showing how to clean many different kinds of stains and keep it in your laundry area.

- Shout Color Guard sheets in the washing machine work great to keep colors from spreading between clothing and cut down on pre-sorting loads.

- Avoid buying children's clothes that require ironing, dry cleaning, hand-washing, or are hang-to-dry only.

Children's Clothing

One chore we all struggle with is managing the mounds of children's clothing that pile up. Between boys and girls, and spans of ages and seasons, it is definitely an area that requires good organization. Without some management strategies, your closets and drawers are at risk of becoming totally out of control, which only makes the morning dressing routine more frustrating. Hopefully you will find a few tips here to help avoid these pitfalls.

STAYING ORGANIZED

- For older children, keep some seasonally neutral clothes in their drawers for in-between seasons. Otherwise, sort clothes and check sizes when you change over their fall/winter and spring/summer wardrobes. Remember that sometimes clothes will fit smaller or larger on a sibling due to wear, shrinkage and stretching.

- Hang outfits together – bottoms with matching tops. This helps young children to pick out their own outfits, and helps you when you're in a hurry.

- Buy only one brand of sock, as it's easier to match when doing laundry if they're all the same. To make it even easier, buy only one color.

- If possible, sort through hand-me-downs before you accept them, and only take what you will realistically use.

- Locate the nearest Salvation Army or Goodwill and teach children to share with those less fortunate.

Store an empty basket near the changing table or dresser, or under the bed, to put clothes in as baby outgrows them. Have sturdy, stackable containers ready to store clothes, labeled by age, size, gender and season.

MAKING DRESSING SIMPLE

- It's easier to dress infants in clothes with snaps rather than buttons. Avoid one-piece outfits that you'll have to pull over their heads.

- Shirts and outfits with collars can be very annoying as they tend to flip up, need ironing, and get dirty easily.

- Overalls are a hassle when it comes to changing diapers or potty training. You either have to take them right off, or you need to unfasten all the little snaps.

- Hanna Andersson moccasin slippers are great – sure to stay on those little feet!

- Roll up shirt sleeves or pant legs BEFORE you put them on your child.

- If children are squirmy when putting on socks and shoes, put them on while they're sitting in their highchair or booster seat.

- Velcro shoes are much easier and quicker to get on than lace up shoes.

- Pants with adjustable or elastic waistbands are more comfortable and last longer.

- Give children two options for clothing, so they feel more independent.

- When you want your children to become more independent in choosing and matching clothing, use colored coat hangers for corresponding tops and bottoms. For example, use the same colored hangers for all tops and pants that go together, and when they pick out an outfit, they only have to choose matching hanger colors.

"Encourage an interest in music
and the arts, as they contribute to both
mental and emotional development."

9. FUN TIME

Fun Indoor Activities

Whether it's a rainy day, a wintry blizzard, or just a lazy afternoon hanging around the house, there are times when you're just pulling your hair out wondering what to do with the kids! Following are some quick and easy suggestions of activities for all ages that you can pull out of your hat to keep them amused for hours.

INFANTS

- Play with bubbles.
- Peek-a-boo with toys under a blanket.
- Water splash time in sink or tub – add bubbles for more fun!
- Put pudding or yogurt on a highchair tray and let them squish around.
- Do a "tour around the world" – go from room to room in the house and explore.
- Play with baby in a mirror.
- Secure ends of a toilet roll and fill it with various items to make different sounds (with supervision).
- Play different kinds of music and dance around.
- Buy the baby booties with rattles in them.
- Play with a ball that you can squish easily.
- Tell stories with puppets.
- Experiment with fabrics of different textures, such as scarves, feathers, and wool.

- Choose different scents for them to smell. For example, spices, soaps, candles.
- Give a baby massage.
- When baby is just about ready to start crawling, take the couch cushions off the couch and place them onto the floor and let them explore up and down.

MAKE YOUR OWN CHALK-BOARD IN THE HOUSE! Purchase chalk paint at your local paint store. With masking tape outline the section you want to fill in. Make sure the area is at the proper height for your child, not you! Presto! You have an instant chalkboard! You have an easy educational tool that has many important benefits including building the muscles in your child's arms for writing and fostering endless creativity.

TODDLERS AND PRESCHOOLERS

These activities can be adapted to suit various ages – use your imagination and have a blast with your kids! (They are also great ideas to leave for a babysitter.)

- Use a blanket or sheet over top of kitchen chairs to make a "rocket ship". Cut out circles for the planets and tape them on the inside then sit inside with a flashlight and pretend you're flying into space.
- Have children help to make homemade play dough, then play with one of many fun play dough sets you can purchase.
- Keep any large boxes you acquire to make a car, train, kitchen, castle, or dollhouse.
- Bowling with empty soda cans.
- Play with washable finger paint in the bathtub for easy cleanup of both child and space.
- Play children's card games, such as old maid, fish, war, crazy 8's.
- Any kind of dancing to music.
- Games such as "ring-around-the-rosie" or "duck, duck goose".
- Sing along CDs, marching, counting or identifying body parts.
- Create a "store" with household objects that kids go shopping for. Have one child be the shopper and one the cashier.
- Make edible necklaces – string fruit loops or cheerios.
- Print coloring and activity pages from the internet, perhaps from a child's favorite TV show website.

- Make an obstacle course in the house, using things like chairs to go under and over, couch cushions to climb over, toys to jump over, or a dress-up outfit to take on and off.
- Baking activities can integrate a lot of learning for preschoolers, such as counting, following directions and fine motor skills.
- Beading – use pipe cleaners for smaller kids, then build up to stretchy cording to make necklaces and bracelets.
- Play a memory game using toys. Show five, have child leave room, remove one, and have them come back and guess what's missing. Take turns guessing.
- Play hide 'n' seek.
- Let them play in the kitchen sink.
- Make up a "Blue's Clues" or "Dora the Explorer" game around the house.
- Make a calendar with family pictures or drawings for each month.
- Turn a coffee table on its side for an instant puppet theater.

ACTIVITY BOX

Kids love rice, sand, dry pasta, and water play. Use a shower curtain liner to lay on the floor to keep mess contained, then just roll it up and dump it back into your containers (except the water, of course!). Shallow under-the-bed wardrobe boxes are perfect containers for storage and floor play.

More Lifesavers

Celebrations

Birthdays are special milestones to celebrate. We want our precious little ones to have the time of their lives! However, for parents it can be overwhelming deciding on a theme and venue, organizing the party, and making sure everyone shows up! We hope to supply you with suggestions and tips to help create a stress-free birthday event that provides wonderful memories for both you and your child!

THEMES

Choosing a birthday theme is usually an easy task, as not only do most children have definite likes and dislikes, but they usually start talking about their birthdays months in advance! There are a lot of ideas out there, some of which include:

- Animal – dog, cat, horses.
- Barnyard – dress like cowboys and cowgirls.
- Beach/pool party – have a slip n' slide, water balloons, sprinklers.
- Circus – do face painting, hire a clown.
- Dinosaur – create an archeological "dig" for dinosaur bones.
- Fall fair – rent a "Moonwalk" for jumping.
- Favorite Disney character.
- Favorite television character or program.
- Hawaiian – complete with lei's and a luau.
- Jungle safari – wear safari hats and "hunt" for animals.
- Magic – hire a magician.
- Medieval – wear knight and princess costumes, rent a pony.
- Mexican fiesta – have a piñata, sombreros, make-your-own tacos.
- Seasonal – apple picking, winter sledding.

For Girls

- Diva – dress-up in shiny outfits and dance the party away.
- Flashback to the 60's, 70's, or 80's! – hippies, disco ball.
- Mermaid – underwater theme with a splash in a kiddie pool.
- Princess – crowns, wands, and pin the lips on the frog game.
- Slumber party – nail painting, popcorn, black lights, pillow fights.
- Tea party – make tiny pastries and finger sandwiches.

For Boys

- Firefighter – wear fire hats and visit a fire station.
- Knights – dress as knights in shining armor, make "horses" out of brooms.
- Outer space – make spaceships out of shipping boxes and tinfoil.
- Pirates – have a treasure hunt.
- Race cars – have matchbox car races.
- Sports – get a favorite theme and hit a "homerun".
- Super heroes.
- Trains (Thomas) – dress up like train conductors with hats and scarves around their necks.

VENUES

Having parties outside of the home can become a costly venture. If your child has their heart set on a certain venue that is expensive, consider having them team up with a friend who has a birthday close to theirs. As long as the birthday children don't mind sharing the glory, this can alleviate some of the expenses and will also provide extra help for you. Lastly, if you have a choice to have the party on a weekday versus the weekend, choose a weekday. There will be fewer crowds and you may ensure a better turnout if you're not encroaching on the guests' family time.

Some questions to consider when choosing a party venue include:

- Has the site hosted birthday parties before?
- Is there a flat fee or is it cost per child? Is there a minimum fee? Deposit required? Is there a rain cancellation party for outdoor sites?
- What is provided – invitations? cake? paper goods? decorations?
- What entertainment is provided, and what are you responsible for?
- Are you expected to provide chaperones?
- Will there be other parties at the same time?
- Can you drop-in on another party prior to booking your own, to see how it's run?
- What is the liability policy in case of injury?
- If you know other parents who have used the location before, ask if the children had a great time and if the venue delivered all that was expected.
- Who's responsible for clean-up?

IDEAS

- "Build-a-Bear" stores.
- "Paint it Yourself" pottery establishment.
- Amusement or water park.
- Bowling alley.
- Children's museum or aquarium.

- Conservation area (Audubon Society locations are great).
- Gym, indoor play establishment, or swim facility.
- Local farm.
- Miniature golf.
- Movie theater.
- Park with outdoor play equipment.
- Zoo.

HELPFUL TIPS FOR AN AWESOME TIME!

- Check out www.birthdaysrus.com for complete planning ideas.
- Great birthday theme packages can be ordered from www.birthdayexpress.com.
- Oriental Trading Company offers inexpensive bulk party favors (www.orientaltrading.com).
- Simple, homemade parties are just as fun for kids and a lot less expensive. Cake and ice cream and a little playtime are a lot of fun for young children.
- If you have a playgroup that celebrates birthdays, group the children together if birthdays are close enough, and just have one party.
- Check around – you can often find someone who has a party business, whereby they will come to your house (you choose from their list of themes) and decorate, run the party, including crafts and cake, and clean up too. All you do is send the invitations!
- Instead of presents, each child could bring an item to be donated. For example, books for a book drive, or teddy bears for a local children's hospital or fire station.
- When children are under four, do not have them open their presents in front of everyone, as it can lead to unnecessary commotion. Be sure to take a picture of your child opening each gift, and then send it along in the thank-you card.
- Be sure your party is at an appropriate time of day – be considerate of nap times.

- Make the parents aware of your party plans. For example, you need to be aware of any children's allergies, or any specific fears that may relate to your chosen theme, such as clowns or masks.
- Enlist the help of friends and family to help you with the children and party preparations.
- Always send a thank-you note!

PARTY FAVOR IDEAS

- Personalized stickers, magnets and buttons with your child's name on them (from www.birthdayinabox.com).
- Small items like stickers, small plastic toys, wrapped candy or snack, decorative pencils, and bubbles are proven winners.
- Give each child a balloon with a small plush animals tied to the bottom to secure the balloon from floating off – it's a party decoration AND a take home party favor.
- Select items that relate to the theme as much as possible. For example, if the party has a cowboy theme, present all the children with a bandana, cowboy hat, and sheriff badge to keep.
- Coordinate a treasure hunt for treat bags. Decorate each bag with a different set of stickers, and put one corresponding sticker on an index card. Hand children a card and have them find the treat bag that matches. This not only provides an extra activity at the party, it emphasizes the fun of the hunt, verses what's IN the bag.

FUN ACTIVITIES

- Engage your excited party-goers immediately with a craft project. This will eliminate a lot of running around.
- The items in a piñata can often be small toys, "jewelry," or figurines if candy isn't desired.
- A small, easy string attachment can be added to a piñata to pull it apart, eliminating the use of a bat if so desired (perfect for the young preschooler).

- Beads and foam stickers are fun.
- Decorate crowns
- Face painting is always a hit!
- As children get older, planning a special day or evening activity with a couple of friends could be just as special as having a big party.
- Hire a clown, magician or musician to perform at your party.
- Paint a plain white "piggy" bank and go on a treasure hunt for coins!
- Rental centers have snow cone and cotton candy machines, for a minimal daily cost.

Make Ice-Cream in a Baggie!

You need:

1/2 cup milk
1/2 cup half and half
1 tbsp sugar
1/4 tsp vanilla extract
2 cups ice
1 tbsp salt
2 sandwich size Ziploc bags
1 one gallon size Ziploc bag
1 hand towel or gloves to keep
   fingers from freezing, too.

What to do:

Put one small Ziploc bag inside another. Add the milk, half and half, sugar, and vanilla to the inside bag. Seal both bags securely, removing excess air. Add 2 cups ice and 1 tbsp salt to large bag. Place small bag inside and seal. Let the kids shake themselves silly. Ice cream will be soft and ready to eat in 5 to 10 minutes.

Crafts

Most children love doing crafts! Activities such as these not only provide your children with tons of fun, they also help to work on many developmental skills. Once you have a craft cupboard stocked and ready to go, it's easy to pull out supplies and let your little DaVinci create!

ORGANIZE THINGS FIRST

Supplies

- Find a closet or a cabinet which you can lock or monitor closely for storing arts and crafts supplies (all paper, crayons, markers, pencils, scissors, paints and glue). For younger children, take out art materials only when you are able to supervise, and put everything away immediately when finished. This helps to avoid things like cutting hair and clothing, marking on walls, rugs, bodies, eating crayons or paints.

- Keep all grown up pencils, pens, scissors, tape and staplers completely out of reach and sight.

- Have separate bins for each child for items such as crayons, markers, and papers. This way there's no fighting over these things, and each child is responsible for cleaning up their own bins after playing.

- Use blunt-tipped scissors under adult supervision, around age three. Kids love to use them and they need experience with them for school. A great way to teach using scissors is to stand behind your child and use your hand to help – it's hard to teach cutting if you're sitting in front of the child.

DISPLAYING MASTERPIECES

- Don't worry if a craft doesn't come out like it's supposed to look - your child made it so it's perfect.

- Put name and date on artwork.

- Try taping artwork together to use as gift wrap.

To display artwork, put two nails in wall and tie string across very tightly, then use clothespins to hold things up. Or, buy corkboard that's flexible and in strips that you can hang across the wall and use pushpins to display masterpieces. Change them over regularly, replacing old with new. If something is worth keeping, frame it using poster frames or some other inexpensive frame you can keep on hand (poster board makes nice matting). Also remember that it's okay to throw out your children's artwork!

CRAFT SUPPLY CHECKLIST

- ☐ Beads and stretchy cording
- ☐ Blunt scissors
- ☐ Buttons
- ☐ Chalkboard with varying sizes of chalk
- ☐ Crayons, colored pencils/sharpener, magic markers (all washable!)
- ☐ Easel with paint cups and lids
- ☐ Fabric remnants and ribbons
- ☐ Feathers
- ☐ Felt
- ☐ Glitter
- ☐ Glitter pens

- ☐ Glue sticks
- ☐ Googly eyes
- ☐ Magazines
- ☐ Old greeting cards
- ☐ Paint pens
- ☐ Paper plates
- ☐ Paper: construction – white large-sized and smaller multi-colored sheets
- ☐ Pipe-cleaners
- ☐ Play dough and harder modeling clay (polymer clay)
- ☐ Pom-poms
- ☐ Popsicle sticks
- ☐ Poster paper and cardboard

- ☐ Scissors that cut a design
- ☐ Shower curtain to use as a drip guard
- ☐ Sponges, rubber stamps and ink pads
- ☐ Stickers, spongy stickers
- ☐ Tin foil and wax paper
- ☐ Tissue paper
- ☐ Uncooked pasta shells and noodles
- ☐ Various sized brushes
- ☐ Washable tempera paint, watercolors and finger-paints
- ☐ White glue
- ☐ Yarn

More Ideas

_____

_____

_____

_____

_____

_____

Recipes for Fun

LICKABLE FINGER PAINT

You need:

1 can condensed milk

food coloring

finger paint paper

What to do:

1. Divide condensed milk into small bowls. Add food coloring and mix to make different colors. (Red, blue and yellow work well to experiment with making new colors.)

2. Lay out finger paint paper and let children have a blast!!

Note:

- For younger children, put a couple of colors of paint in a large Ziploc bag, sealed and reinforced with duct or masking tape.

- Place bag on highchair or table and have children "draw" with their fingers for a great mess-free activity!

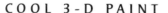

COOL 3-D PAINT

You need:

1/2 cup white glue

1/2 cup white shaving cream

food coloring

What to do:

1. Mix the glue and shaving cream in a bowl.

2. Divide into two or three smaller bowls, and mix in a few drops of food coloring to create different colors.

3. Let sit for a few minutes, then use as paint to create 3-D pictures!

Note:

- You can make paint colorful by adding a few drops of food coloring.

- Use foam balls to make snowmen.

- Add glitter of coconut for special effect.

SCRATCH 'N SNIFF PAINT

You need:

Kool-Aid
(different flavors)

paint

paper

What to do:

1. Add dry Kool-Aid drink crystals to slightly dilute (with water) paint (about 1 tsp. to half a baby food jar of diluted paint). The diluted paint gives a wonderful watercolor effect!

2. Have children paint pictures, and when they're dry, scratch and sniff the paint! Try matching scents to colors, such as strawberry red paint, grape purple paint, etc.

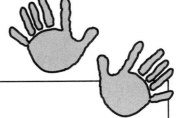

FINGER PAINT

You need:

1 envelope
unflavored gelatin

1/2 cup cornstarch

3 tbsp sugar

2 cups cold water

food coloring

dishwashing liquid

white shelf paper

What to do:

1. Soak gelatin in 1/4 cup warm water and set aside.

2. Mix cornstarch and sugar in medium-sized pot.

3. Gradually add remaining water and cook slowly over slow heat, stirring until well blended.

4. Remove from heat and add gelatin.

5. Divide into containers and add a drop or two of dishwashing liquid and food coloring into each.

SIDEWALK PAINT

You need:

1/2 cup cornstarch

1/2 cup cold water

6-8 drops food coloring

What to do:

1. Mix cornstarch and water into small plastic bowl.

2. Stir in food coloring.

3. Repeat to create different colors of paint.

4. Paint on sidewalk – it washes easily away with water!

COLORED MACARONI BEADS

You need:

food coloring

rubbing alcohol

dry macaroni that make good beads

stretchy cord for stringing beads

What to do:

1. Place macaroni in a bowl and sprinkle with several drops of food coloring and a splash of rubbing alcohol.
2. Mix well and spread on cookie sheet to dry.
3. Have kids string up into necklaces and bracelets.

BLOW PAINT PICTURES

You need:

straws

paint

paper

What to do:

1. Pour a small amount of paint in middle of paper.
2. Have children take a straw and blow the paint around, creating a modern-looking work of art!

Note: Not for younger children, as you don't want them to drink the paint.

COLORED POPCORN PICTURES

You need:

1 cup popped popcorn

2 tbsp water

5-7 drops food coloring

large Ziploc bag

white glue

What to do:

1. Put popcorn in bag.
2. Mix water and food coloring and pour on top of the popcorn.
3. Close bag and shake until popcorn turns color.
4. Pour popcorn out onto a paper towel to dry.
5. Glue popcorn onto paper to create a picture.

SOAP BUBBLE PICTURES

You need:

aluminum pie plate

1 cup bubble solution

1/2 cup tempera paint

copier or light-colored construction paper

plastic drinking straws

What to do:

1. Mix bubbles and paint in aluminum pie plate.
2. Blow mixture with straw until bubbles mound up in plate.
3. Just as the bubbles begin to overflow, gently touch paper to the bubbles.
4. Repeat until paper is covered or design is created.

Note: Use several pie plates, each with a different color, and mix the colors in a picture.

COLORED SALT PICTURES

You need:

1 cup table salt

2 tsp powdered tempera paint

baggies

white glue or glue stick

paper

What to do:

1. Pour salt and powdered paint into baggies.
2. Close tightly and shake bag until color is completely blended.
3. Make as many different colors as you like.
4. Draw a picture using either the white glue or a glue stick.
5. Pour the desired colored salt over different areas of the picture to create a colorful picture.

COOL WHIP ART

You need:

Cool Whip

food coloring

heavy paper

What to do:

1. Mix food coloring into Cool Whip to get desired colors. (HINT: don't add too much or it will be runny, and don't over mix it.)
2. Put dollops of Cool Whip on paper and "create' with hands, paint brushes, etc.
3. Dry flat on a table to make creative 3-D pictures!

HOMEMADE CHALK

You need:

1 cup plaster of paris

1/2 cup water

2-3 tbsp tempera paint

molds: can use candy molds, paper cups, toilet paper tubes with tinfoil at end, muffin tins

What to do:

1. Mix plaster of paris and paint.
2. Add water and mix well.
3. Pour into molds and let dry for 24 hours.
4. Remove from mold and let air dry for 2-7 days, depending on size.

Note: Make sparkly chalk by adding 1 tsp glitter into the plaster mixture.

RECYCLED CRAYONS

You need:

broken crayons

muffin tin

paper muffin liners

What to do:

1. Peel paper from broken crayons
2. Place individual crayon pieces into muffin tray
3. Melt in a warm oven (about 200 degrees) until melted.
4. Cool and pop new crayons out of paper liner.

Note: You can use many different molds like ice cube trays in different shapes, candy molds, and silicon muffin trays to make crayon removal easy.

TISSUE PAPER ART

You need:

1" squares of different colored tissue paper

glue

craft paper

pencil

What to do:

1. Roll tissue paper into little balls, dab in glue, and place on paper.
2. Younger children can place the balls on glue spots you place on paper, and older children can create their own picture with the tissue balls. (Makes great flowers!)
3. You can also wrap the tissue squares around the end of a pencil and glue them on the paper.

COFFEE FILTER FLOWERS

You need:

coffee filters

crayola markers

shallow bowl with water

pipe cleaners

What to do:

1. Draw a pattern on, or color the coffee filter with the markers.
2. Fold the filter into a cone shape, and lay the tip into a bowl of shallow water.
3. Watch as the water travels up the filter and spreads the color.
4. Allow the filters to dry.
5. Use pipe cleaners to attach to the center of the filter to make the flowers stem.

PAINTED ROCKS

You need:

poster/tempera paint

smooth, flat rocks

small rocks, odds and ends

Elmer's glue

What to do:

1. Wash the rock and let dry.
2. Paint the rock.
3. With glue, add small rocks for eyes and legs. Add "odds and ends" to create your creature.

JIGSAW PUZZLE

You need:

glue stick

poster Board

one full page of a desired picture (try "zoo books", a nature magazine, or even a photo)

What to do:

1. Glue picture to poster board.
2. When glue is dry, cut the picture into various shapes to make puzzle pieces.

PLAY DOUGH (COOKED)

You need:
1 cup water
1 cup flour
1/2 cup salt
2 tbsp. vegetable oil
2 tbsp. cream of tartar
food coloring

What to do:
1. Mix everything together.
2. Cook on medium heat for 10 – 15 minutes.
3. Knead dough 10 times. Let cool.
4. Add food coloring after it's cooled.

JELL-O PLAY DOUGH

You need:
4 cups flour
1 cup salt
2 pkgs. unsweetened jell-o
4 tsp cream of tartar

What to do:
1. Mix above ingredients together, then add:
2. 2 cups boiling water
3. 2 tsp cooking oil
4. Mix together well and knead until desired consistency.

AIR DRY CLAY

You need:
3 cups flour
1 cup salt
1/2 cup white glue
1 cup water
1 tsp lemon juice

What to do:
1. Mix together until well-blended.
2. Mold into shapes, or roll out and cut with cookie cutters.
3. Let dry overnight, then paint.

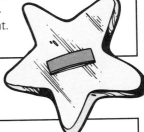

CINNAMON CLAY

You need:
1/4 cup white glue
1/3 cup applesauce
3 tbsp cinnamon
1 3/4 cups flour
1/4 cup water

What to do:
1. Mix ingredients together until dough forms a ball.
2. Knead for a few minutes, adding flour as needed.
3. Make into desired shapes or roll out and cut with cookie cutters.
4. Bake at 300 degrees for 10 minutes.
5. Makes great ornaments.

ICE SUN CATCHERS

You need:

aluminum pie plate

pictures, such as scenery, cold weather, sports, polar bears, penguins, or anything at all.

hammer and nail

string

What to do:

1. Freeze 1" of water in an aluminum pie plate.
2. Dampen pictures with water. Put on ice in pie plate.
3. Cover with 1" of water, and re-freeze.
4. Remove sun catcher from pie plate.
5. With warm nail pierce a hole to thread a string for hanging.
6. Hang outside a window and watch it glitter!

SNOWMAN

You need:

1 baby food jar, or jar with lid

1" styrofoam ball

1 toothpick

orange marker

fine black marker

hot chocolate mix

small candy cane

mini marshmallows

glue gun

scrap felt or fleece

What to do:

1. Fill jar half full of hot chocolate mix.
2. Add mini marshmallows. Screw on lid.
3. With glue gun (or tacky glue) glue Styrofoam head onto the lid and set aside to dry.
4. Color the toothpick orange, and break in half.
5. Stick the toothpick in the Styrofoam head to make a nose.
6. With black marker make eyes and a smile.
7. Cut a narrow strip of felt/fleece long enough to tie like a scarf. Fringe the ends. Wrap around neck of jar.
8. Hook the candy cane on the scarf.

Note: This craft can be modified to suit the season, holiday, or event.

VARIATIONS:

Clown

1. Fill jar with jelly beans.
2. Decorate head to look like a clown.
3. Add a ruffled piece of lace to look like a collar.

Jac'o Lantern

1. Fill jar with orange drink mix.
2. Color Styrofoam ball orange.
3. Add black eyes, mouth and nose to look like a jack'o lantern.

GLITTER

You need:

food coloring

1/2 cup salt

wax paper

What to do:

1. Mix together 5-6 drops food coloring and salt, stir well.
2. Cook in microwave for 1-2 minutes.
3. Spread out on a piece of waxed paper to air-dry then store in airtight container.

SLIME

You need:

2 cups white glue

2 cups water

food coloring

1 tsp. borax

What to do:

1. Pour glue into a mixing bowl.
2. Slowly add 1 1/2 cups of water and a few drops of food coloring.
3. In another bowl, dissolve borax in 1/2 cup of water.
4. Add dissolved borax to glue mixture. Knead about 10 minutes, until slime separates between your fingers. Let slime condense in an airtight container overnight before using.

Note:

Stores for up to 2 weeks in an airtight container.

This is NOT edible!

GOO

You need:

1/2 cup white glue

1 cup cornstarch

food coloring

mixing bowl

cutting board

metal spoon

plastic baggie

What to do:

1. Mix glue and starch together in a bowl.
2. Add in desired food coloring – consistency should become stiff but runny when picked up. (If too runny, add more starch.)
3. Begin to knead it with your hands on your cutting board. (Just like kneading bread dough.)
4. Store in an airtight plastic baggie or container for up to 3 weeks.

BOUNCEABLE CRAZY PUTTY

You need:

3/4 cup white glue

liquid starch

food coloring

What to do:

1. Add enough liquid starch to white glue until a ball is formed.
2. Add food coloring and knead dough until completely worked in.

THE BEST BUBBLES

You need:

2 1/2 quarts water

1/2 cup light corn syrup

1 cup liquid detergent

What to do:

1. Mix water and corn syrup until well blended.
2. Gently stir in dish detergent.
3. Will store several weeks in an airtight container.

SUPER BUBBLES

You need:

1/2 cup store-bought bubbles

1/2 cup liquid dish detergent

2 tbsp. sugar

What to do:

1. Mix together until sugar dissolves.
2. Pour in shallow trays, or plastic cups, and use regular bubble maker tools to make huge bubbles.

COLORED BUBBLES

You need:

1 cup granulated soap or soap powder

1 quart warm water

food coloring

What to do:

1. Dissolve soap in warm water.
2. Stir in food coloring.

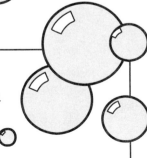

Toys

Who doesn't like to play? Even adults need to find time to enjoy activities to stay out of the daily drudge. Did you know that kids NEED to play to develop the skills necessary to learn and be a productive adult? Play incorporates many developmental areas: it involves the skills of exploration, experimentation, and the ability to ask questions. Play is vital in developing motor, cognitive, language, emotional, and social skills. Play is a child's work.

Children usually do not need any encouragement to play – it's in their genes to do so, and offering an environment in which to play safely is vital. Independence grows as a child embraces their surroundings and investigates the possibilities of life. In play, the world is their oyster – from battling imaginary fires with a red fire hat and garden hose, to mastering a multi-piece puzzle. Offer toys that leave room for creativity and imaginations to burst forth and while they are at it, join in and have some fun, too!

WHAT TO LOOK FOR

- Look for toys with lots of uses.
- Good, simple, old-fashioned toys allow creativity and individuality.
- Choose toys carefully and don't keep anything that you don't want to pick up until children are old enough and willing to clean up themselves.
- For children under 3, avoid small parts that may be a choking hazard. A good rule of thumb is the toilet paper roll test. If an item can fit into the hole of a toilet paper roll freely, then it is too small for a young child.
- For electronic toys, check batteries regularly for corrosion.

TIPS TO KEEP TOYS ORGANIZED

- Have an out-of-sight place (closet or high shelves) to store most toys and only leave a few at a time out for children to use.
- Cycle out current toys before adding something new. This will make pick-up easier, and children won't become distracted by too many choices.
- Keep toys with a lot of pieces contained together in a separate box or bin, preferably with a lid. Large Ziploc bags are also great for organization.
- Regularly "clean house" and give toys away to charity or swap with a friend.
- If you have a second baby, it's time to put toys with small pieces away. Put them in a container on a high shelf and let the older child play with them while the baby is napping.
- For great advice on toys and many other children's products, go to the Oppenheim Toy Portfolio for a current "best of" list at www.toyportfolio.com.

BABY'S FIRST YEAR (0-12 MONTHS)

- Bouncy seat with fixed toy attachments
- Brightly colored cloth balls or rubber textured balls that can be easily grasped
- Cloth books
- Educational toys from the Whoozit Company
- Exersaucers
- Jolly jumper
- Leap Frog Learning Table
- Musical and moving mobiles
- Ocean Wonders Aquarium for the crib
- Overhead activity gym
- Peek-a-boo blocks (see-through blocks with objects inside them)
- Round-About ball game
- Smooth plastic or soft toys that can be chewed
- Stacking rings
- Unbreakable large handled rattles
- Washable soft dolls and stuffed animals

1 YEAR

- Band Away Boat (Discovery Toys)
- Blocks (large building blocks)
- Board books
- Fisher Price little people and play sets
- Gertie balls by Small World Toys. They are soft balls of varying sizes, textures and colors.
- Indoor plastic slide, if you have the space
- Magical push walker, once walking starts
- Non-glass mirrors
- Phonics Radio by Leap Frog
- Photo albums

- Push and pull toys
- Sandbox
- Shape sorter
- Stacking cups
- Take-apart toys with large pieces
- Xylophone

2 YEARS

- Animal sets, including dinosaurs, knights and horses
- Beach balls
- Busy box
- Child size table and chairs
- Duplo blocks
- Fisher Price Pop-Onz blocks
- Items that assist in identifying color, size and shapes
- Low rocking horse
- Outdoor swing set
- Peg boards
- Petite kitchen and accessories (play food and pots and pans)
- Play-Skool See & Say
- Puzzles with large pieces and handles (Melissa & Doug Company make nice ones)
- Ride-on toys, such as wagons and tricycles
- Set up a nursery for baby dolls with a stroller, clothing, blankets and bottles
- Silk fabric for a multitude of uses such as costumes, forts, and creative play
- Simple musical instruments
- Tape recorder with cassette tapes and a microphone
- Telephone that makes noise when buttons are pressed
- Toy vehicles
- Train set with table

3 YEARS

- Action figures
- Camera
- Construction sets with easily connecting pieces
- Doctor and other role playing sets
- Doll house with accessories
- Dolls with wrap around clothing
- Etch-a-Sketch
- Inertia toys made of wood such as ramps and small cars
- K'nex construction sets
- Large rubber ball with a handle to bounce on
- Leap Pad computer – it can be a great alone or together activity
- Legos
- Magnadoodle
- Magnetic ABC's for refrigerator or metal cookie sheet
- Matchbox cars
- Mr. Potato Head with Spud in a carrying case
- Play-Doh and accessories
- Puppet theater with puppets
- Radio Flyer wagon with two seats and seatbelts
- Simple card and board games (Candyland, Lucky Ducks, Memory, and color and shape matching games)

- Tea set
- Teach to dress myself toy
- Trikes – always use a bicycle helmet
- Wooden play food set you can "cut"

4 YEARS

- Activity books
- Bicycle with 20 inch wheels, and training wheels with helmet
- Bingo games, such as "Zingo"
- Cut out paper dolls
- Felt boards
- Flash cards
- Kites
- Lite-brite
- Magneatos by Guidecraft (large magnets you build with)
- More demanding board games and card games
- More elaborate dress-up play
- Polly Pockets
- Race cars and remote control cars
- Ravensburger puzzles and games
- Sewing cards
- Sporting equipment, such as a basketball net or t-ball set
- Stencils
- Three wheel scooter, along with elbow and knee pads and a helmet

More Ideas

_____

_____

_____

_____

_____

_____

10. SAFETY

In Safe Hands

Providing a safe environment for your children to live and play in is crucial. Your house, both inside and out, is chock-full of dangers to naturally curious and impulsive children. It is your responsibility to ensure the necessary preparations involved in making your home and family as safe as possible. A good way to start is to take Red Cross certified first aid and CPR classes, which will provide potentially life saving skills in event of an emergency.

PRECAUTIONS FOR INFANTS

- Lay babies on their backs for naps and sleeping.
- Be careful where you leave your baby in the car or bouncy seat. Never place on top of tables or counter tops.
- Never leave baby unattended while in a swing.
- Don't use baby walkers – they're very dangerous around stairs and thresholds.
- Always supervise infants when around older siblings and pets.
- Don't let your baby lie in a beanbag chair.
- Don't let baby nap on a couch or armchair.
- Always use a safety strap when changing a baby on a changing table, or keep a firm hand on the baby at all times. Never leave the baby unattended, and have supplies within your reach.
- Keep changing supplies out of baby's reach. Don't allow baby to grab powder or baby oil, as their lungs can become severely injured if powder is inhaled or oil is swallowed.
- The First Candle/SIDS Alliance promotes infant health and survival during the prenatal period through 2 years. (www.firstcandle.com)

CRIBS

- Slats of crib should be no wider than 2 3/8 inches apart.
- Be weary of older cribs which may not meet current safety standards and may have been painted with lead paint.
- Never lay the baby on a pillow to go to sleep.
- Make sure baby cannot reach mobiles hanging from above.

- Use a crib bumper for babies, making sure ties hang outside the crib and aren't longer than 6 inches.
- As soon as your child can sit or stand, lower the mattress to the lowest possible level. Keep things out of the crib that they could stack to climb on top of and fall out, including crib bumpers, large toys, and stuffed animals.
- When your child can climb out of the crib, put them on a mattress on the floor, in a toddler bed, or in a regular bed with bedrails.
- If you're having trouble keeping your child contained in their room, put a gate in the doorway.

IN THE KITCHEN

- Remove stove dials from the burners if they're on the front, and keep pot handles turned in while cooking.
- Keep all household cleaners in a cabinet with a childproof lock.
- Keep cooking oils locked up as well, as children can become dangerously sick if oil is swallowed and enters the lungs.
- For cabinets that aren't locked, store safe things like Tupperware and pots and pans.
- When you're finished using your oven, don't leave the door open to let the heat out.
- Don't get distracted while you're cooking, as you can easily burn pots and dinners you just worked hard on. If you need to leave the stove while cooking, turn off the burners.
- Never hold a child while cooking by a stove or drinking a hot beverage.

IN THE BATHROOM

- Make sure the hot water heater is set at 120 degrees F or lower to avoid scalding (48 degrees C).
- Keep the bathroom door closed when not in use.
- When filling a bathtub, always run the cold water first and then add hot to make it warm, so that hot water is never running into the tub.
- Always test bathwater before placing your child into the bathtub. Purchase a heat sensing Ducky to alert you to hot bathwater.
- Use non-slip strips or a bathmat in the bathtub, and use a faucet protector to avoid bumped heads.
- Never leave children unattended in the tub. It is too easy to get distracted with a phone call or a news report on the TV, and it only takes a second for an accident to occur.
- Remember a child can drown in less than 1" of water.
- Once the kids are taken out of the bathtub, drain water immediately.
- Always keep the toilet lid closed.
- Keep all medicines up high and in locked cabinets.
- Unplug and store hair dryers, curling irons, and razors when not using them.
- Be aware of what you throw in the trash that kids can get into, such as disposable razors, lids from shampoo bottles and batteries.
- Keep all bathroom and toiletry products in a cabinet with a childproof lock.

IN GENERAL AROUND THE HOUSE

- Use outlet covers, doorknob covers, corner guards on tables, safety locks on cabinets and drawers, doorway gates, and stair gates. Do not use pressure-mounted gates at the TOP of a staircase – make sure it's bolted to the wall.
- Put a soft guard around fireplace hearth, and a barrier around wood burning stoves.
- Bolt dressers, shelves, and TV stands to wall.
- Position beds away from windows.
- Keep window blind cords wrapped up high.
- Open windows from the TOP, and place window guards in second and third story windows to avoid children pushing on screens and falling out.
- Make sure children are NEVER able to access any cooling fans, as little fingers can often squeeze between the barriers.
- Keep all breakables out of reach and remove top-heavy objects that can be pulled over, such as lamps.
- Don't use area rugs or slippery mats that are easy to trip over.
- Avoid putting a coffee table in the middle of the room. If you are going to use one consider a cushion-top or an ottoman.
- Keep plants put up and out of reach.
- Keep alcoholic beverages in a cabinet with a childproof lock.
- Keep all matches, lighters, and flammables up high in a locked cabinet.
- Have working smoke and carbon dioxide alarms on each floor of the house and check their batteries often.
- Be careful with hot beverages around children.
- Always keep your external doors locked, including attic and basement doors.
- If possible, avoid use of bi-fold doors in the house, which children will constantly be pinching their fingers in, or buy locks for them.

- Be careful where you store things that children could get wrapped around their necks, such as neckties, belts, bathrobes with ties, handbags and measuring tapes.
- Be very careful of items that small children can crawl into and become trapped, such as hope chests, toy boxes, trunk of car, and washing machine.
- Have an easy to locate, fully stocked first-aid kit in the house, replacing items as needed.
- Keep a list of emergency phone numbers posted near each telephone, including poison control center and pediatrician's office.

Put everything away and take it all back out when they go to college!

CHOKING HAZARDS

- If an object can fit into a toilet paper roll, then it is too small and thus a choking hazard for young children.
- Be VERY careful of small things that can go into the mouth. Kids can even choke on a small Band-Aid placed on their knee.
- Don't put small children to bed wearing jewelry or hair accessories.
- Some foods that are choking hazards for children under 4 years old include raisins, hot dogs, raw carrots, celery, grapes, nuts, hard candies, gum, popcorn, raw pears and apples.
- The tabs inside the handles of plastic grocery bags are very dangerous, as they can cling to a child's throat if swallowed and cause choking.
- Always tie all plastic bags in a knot, to avoid kids putting them over their heads.
- Don't let young children play with balloons, and never let any child try to blow up a balloon.

OUTSIDE THE HOME

- Display neon "Kid Alert" sign on the road in front of your house alerting traffic to the fact that you have children playing, and put a "Kidsafe Driveway Guard" across your driveway if children are playing.
- Put 6 inches of playground mulch or pea stone around your swing set, in order to cushion falls and help to prevent broken bones.
- Fence in your yard, if possible.
- Check your yard for poisonous plants (plants are a leading cause of poisoning in preschoolers). Teach your child to never pick or eat ANY plant or berry without your permission.
- Be very careful if using pesticides or herbicides. Always read labels for safety information and follow the proper safety guidelines.
- Have your children wear a bright and colorful clothing so that you can more easily identify them in a park, playground, or at the beach.
- When shopping, don't rely on your child to stay nearby. Always keep a close watch on them.
- Teach your child to answer you if you're calling them. Small children may hide and not say anything if they wander away from you.
- If you have a pet that is kept on a long leash, monitor children closely so they don't trip or get strangled by the cord, and keep it tightly wrapped up when not in use.
- Teach your child not to run and to stand very still if they are approached by a dog. Get to know what dogs live in the neighborhood and which ones are friendly.
- If you use a backyard "kiddie" pool your children require constant supervision and the pool must be emptied and stored upside down when not in use.
- Keep a first aid kit in your car for emergencies on the road or when you are out and about.
- NEVER leave children (or pets) in a car on a warm or hot day, whether it's to continue a nap, or even just for a few minutes. Interior car temperatures rise to dangerous levels very quickly.

CAR SEATS

The safest place to seat your child is in the middle of the back seat, never in front of an air bag. Eighty percent of child car seats are currently installed and are being used incorrectly. A simple thing you can do to ensure the utmost safety for your child in the event of an accident is to have your seats checked by a professional to guarantee proper installation. Visit a child safety seat inspection station, or a certified child passenger safety technician. To find one near you, visit www.seatcheck.com, www.nhtsa.dot.gov, or contact your local police station.

EMERGENCY SITUATIONS

- Have fire extinguishers available on all levels of house.
- Be prepared for a power outage at all times – have flashlights with working batteries on all levels of the house, easily accessible.
- Have a plan if your home loses its heat and electricity. Do you have a fireplace? Stock of wood? A place you can go to warm up?
- Use a heating company that will prioritize your service call because you have small children in the home.
- Know of and be prepared for local area hazards, such as tornadoes or hurricanes, and familiarize yourself with evacuation plans and local area shelters.
- Have a fire escape plan and PRACTICE it with your children, both during the day and night. Make sure everyone knows where to meet.
- Have fire escape rope ladders available near upper floor windows.

A SPECIAL NOTE ON SWIMMING

According to the US Product Safety Commission, drowning is the fourth leading cause of death in children under five years old, with the incidence being even higher in year-round warm weather states. You can never be too safe with children who are exposed to water, including pools, lakes, and the ocean. Most children love being in and around water, but are not aware of their limitations. Have a strict set of water safety rules, and follow them explicitly. Ensure that people who may be watching your children around water are also well versed in these precautions.

POOL SAFETY TIPS

- Start your children in swimming lessons at a young age.
- Make sure all children and adults who swim in your pool are aware of, and follow, the pool rules.
- Children must be constantly supervised.
- Safety features such as pool alarms, alarm bracelets, and an alarm on doors leading to the pool area are important.
- Pool accessories not being used should be kept out of the pool, to avoid enticing children to go in after them.
- Try to have a cordless phone by the pool, both for emergencies and to avoid running back into the house.
- Ensure that floating devices do not give a false sense of security or safety to you or your child.
- All adults in the house should be CPR certified.
- At public pools or beaches, don't rely on lifeguards to watch your children, as these are often busy places and only YOU can provide the necessary supervision.

Literature for Children

"Children are made readers on the laps of their parents." – Emilie Buchwald

Reading to your children is one of the most rewarding gifts you can give them. With the rapid development that occurs in the first few year of life, even babies will benefit from singing, nursery rhymes, and daily story time. These experiences lay the foundation for learning to read later in life. Set time aside each day for quiet reading time with your children. The benefits will come in the form of children who are happy, eager readers.

The American Library Association

The American Library Association promotes many ways parents can help to raise a good reader. Some of their suggestions include:

➡ Right from birth, start reading daily.
➡ Sing songs and nursery rhymes.
➡ Choose simple board books with colorful pictures.
➡ Hold the book so they can see the pictures easily.
➡ Let babies hold and play with books.
➡ Read with lots of expression, or use your own words.
➡ Visit the library regularly and participate in story times.
➡ Have toddlers point to pictures, repeat words, and talk about the story.
➡ Ask them questions about the story.
➡ Read and re-read their favorite parts over and over.
➡ If you have older children, have them read to the younger ones.
➡ Set a good example by having your children see YOU reading a book.
➡ Tell stories about your own family, culture and history.

INFANT BOOK SELECTIONS

Most versions are now available in boardbooks, a MUST with little ones!

- "Big Baby Book" by Helen Oxenbury
- "Dog Food" and "Baby Food" by Saxton Freymann, and Joost Elffers
- "Everyone's Noisy" by Ed Vere
- "Good Night Moon" by Margaret Wise Brown
- "I Kissed the Baby!" by Mary Murphy
- "My Big Book of Everything" by Roger Priddy
- "On the Day you were Born" by Debra Frasier
- "Pat the Bunny" by Dorothy Kunhardt
- "Ten Little Ladybugs" by Melanie Gerth
- "Whoozit Lots and Lots of Love" a soft picture book to insert your own photos

INFANT AND TODDLER AUTHORS AND BOOK SERIES

- Dr. Seuss
- Eric Carle
- Baby Einstein
- "Maisy" by Lucy Cousins
- "My First…"(ABC'c, Pets) DK Publishing (www.dk.com)
- Usborne

TODDLER BOOKS

- "Brown Bear, Brown Bear, What Do You See" by Bill Martin, Jr.
- "Brown Paper Teddy Bear" by Catherine Allison
- "Chicka-Chicka Boom Boom" by Bill Martin, Jr. et al
- "Disney: My First 1000 Words: A Picture Wordbook" by Disney Learning
- "Fuzzy Bear's Potty Book" by Dawn Bentley
- "Good Night, Monkey Boy" and "Bubble Bath Pirates" by Jarrett Krosoczka
- "How do Dinosaurs Say Good Night?" by Jane Yolen and Mark Teague
- "HUG" by Jez Alborough
- "If You Give a Moose a Muffin" by Laura Joffe Numeroff
- "Little Gorilla" by Ruth Bonstein
- "Milo and the Magic Stones" by Marcus Pfister
- "Nat, Nat The Nantucket Cat" by Peter W. Barnes and Cheryl Shaw Barnes
- "Owl Moon" by Jane Yolen
- "The Feel Good Book" by Todd Parr
- "The Little Mouse, The Red Ripe Strawberry, and The Big Hungry Bear" by Don and Audrey Wood
- "The Runaway Bunny" by Margaret Wise Brown
- "The Water Hole" by Graeme Base
- "Tiny Turtles" by Wendy McLean
- "Tumble Bumble" by Felicia Bond

More Ideas

PRESCHOOL AUTHORS AND BOOK SERIES

- Jan Brett
- "Angelina Ballerina" by Katherine Holabird
- "I Spy" by Jean Marzollo
- "Madeline" by Ludwig Bemelmans
- "Magic Tree House" by Mary Pope Osborne
- "Miss Spiders" by Davis Kirk
- "Olivia" by Ian Falconer
- Arthur
- Berenstain Bears
- Clifford
- Curious George
- "Eyewitness Books" by DK Publishing

PRESCHOOL BOOKS

- "A Fish Out of Water" by Helen Palmer and P.D. Eastman
- "I'm a Manatee" by John Lithgow
- "Lost in the Woods" by Carl R. Sams II and Jean Stoick
- "Love You Forever" by Robert Munsch
- "Make Way for Ducklings" by Robert McCloskey
- "Moonbeam" and "Starbright" by Maureen Garth
- "People" by Peter Spier
- "Rainbow Fish" by Marcus Pfister
- "Strega Nona" by Tomie dePaola
- "Swimmy" and "Frederick" by Leo Lionni
- "Thanks and Giving: All Year Long" by Marlo Thomas
- "The Children's Treasury of Classic Poetry" by Nicola Baxter
- "The Giving Tree" by Shel Silverstein
- "The Little Red Hen" by Paul Galdone
- "The Mitten and The Umbrella" by Jan Brett
- "The Napping House" by Audrey Wood
- "The Ugly Truckling" by David Gordon
- "The Velveteen Rabbit" by Margery Williams
- "Whoever You Are" by Mem Fox

GOOD MAGAZINES SUBSCRIPTIONS FOR KIDS

- Highlights
- Preschool Playroom
- Ranger Rick
- Sesame Street
- Turtle
- Wild Animal
- Zoo Books

CHILDREN'S BOOK CATALOGS AND SITES

- Barefoot Books (www.barefootbooks.com)
- Daedalus Children's Books (www.salebooks.com)
- Scholastic Book Club (www.scholastic.com)
- A comprehensive lists of books and learning to read sites are located at www.embracingthechild.org.
- A great parent resource on early literacy can be found on the Reading is Fundamental website (www.RIF.org).

An enduring way to let your children know how much you love them is to inscribe the books you buy for them with words from your heart. If you give a poetry book for example, you can express what you hope poetry will mean to them as they grow up, or what a particular poem meant to you when you were their age. Depending on the book's contents, you can write something funny or silly, or serious and emotional. Such personal thoughts are wonderful expressions of your love for your children. It is fun to read them later and remember what you were thinking at the time. Your children will treasure these inscriptions from the heart and may enjoy reading them as much as the books themselves!

Literature for Parents

PREGNANCY

- "Conception, Pregnancy and Birth" by Dr. Miriam Stoppard
- "Girlfriends Guide to Pregnancy" by Vicki Iovine
- "The Pregnancy Book" by Dr. William Sears and Martha Sears
- "What to Expect… " series by Heidi Murkoff
- "Your Pregnancy Week by Week" by Glade C. Curtis
- "A Good Birth, A Safe Birth : Choosing and Having the Childbirth Experience You Want" by Diana Korte and Roberta Scaer
- "Mothering the Mother : How a Doula Can Help You Have a Shorter, Easier, and Healthier Birth" by Marshall H. Klaus and Phyllis H. Klaus

NURSING

- "Nursing Mother, Working Mother" by Gale Pryor
- "So That's What They're For!" by Janet Tamaro
- "The Nursing Mother's Companion" and "The Nursing Mother's Guide to Weaning" by Kathleen Huggins
- "Womanly Art of Breastfeeding" by Le Leche League

BABY CARE

"Baby Whisperer" by Tracy Hogg and Melinda Blau

- "The Baby Book: Everything You Need to Know about Your Baby from Birth to Age Two" by Dr. William Sears
- "The Good House Keeping Books on Child Care and Pregnancy & Baby Care" by Hearst Books, New York

- "The Happiest Baby on the Block: The New Way to Calm Crying and Help Your Newborn Baby Sleep Longer" by Harvey Karp
- "Your Baby's First Year Week by Week" by Dr. Glade C. Curtis and Judith Schuler

DISCIPLINE

- "1-2-3 Magic" by Thomas Phelan
- "Boundaries for Kids" and "Raising Great Kids" by Drs. Henry Cloud & John Townsend
- "Grace-Based Parenting" by Dr. Tim Kimmel
- "How to Behave So Your Preschooler Will, Too" by Sal Severe
- "Kids are Worth It" by Barbara Colorosa
- "Raising Your Spirited Child" by Mary Sheedy Kurcinka
- "Setting Limits with your Strong-Willed Child" by Robert MacKenzie
- "The Five Love Languages of Children" by Gary Chapman
- "The New Dare to Discipline" and "Bringing up Boys" by Dr. James Dobson

FOOD

- "30-Minute Meals" by Rachel Ray
- "365 Foods Kids Love to Eat" by Sheila Ellison and Judith Gray
- "Better Baby Food– America's Complete Source" and "Better Food for Kids" by Daina Kalnins and Joanne Saab
- "Child of Mine" by Ellyn Slater
- "Mommy Made: Home Cooking for a Healthy Baby and Toddler" by Martha and David Kimmel
- "Quick Meals for Healthy Kids and Busy Parents" by Sandra K. Nissenberg
- "The Family Nutrition Book" by William Sears and Martha Sears
- "The Super Baby Food Diet" by Ruth Yaron

REFERENCE GUIDES

- "1001 Activities for Kids in Tight Spaces" by Carol S. Kranowitz
- "Baby and Child Care" by Dr. Benjamin Spock
- "Birth to Five" by Penelope Leach
- "Caring for Your Baby and Young Child Ages Birth to 5 Years" by American Academy of Pediatrics Staff, et al.
- "From First Kicks to First Steps" by Dr. Alan Greene
- "Honey for a Child's Heart" by Gladys Hunt
- "Siblings Without Rivalry – How to Help your Children Live Together so you can Live Too" and "How to Talk So Kids will Listen and Listen So Kids Will Talk" by Adele Faber and Elaine Mazlish
- "The Child with Special Needs" by Stanley Greenspan
- "The Complete Marriage and Family Home Reference Guide" by Dr. James Dobson
- "Touchpoints" by T. Berry Brazelton, MD

INSPIRATION

- "Chocolate for a Mother's Heart" by Kay Allenbaugh
- "Giving the Love that Heals – A Guide for Parents" by Harville Hendrix and Helen Hunt
- "The 10 Greatest Gifts I Give My Children" by Steven W. Vannoy
- "What Kids Need Most in a Mom" by Patricia H. Rushford
- Bible or other spiritual literature

POSTPARTUM

- "Down Came the Rain: My Journey through Postpartum Depression" by Brooke Shields
- "Mothering the New Mother: Your Postpartum Resource Companion" by Sally Placksin
- "Postpartum Survival Guide" by Anne Dunnewold, Ph.D. and Diane G. Sandford, Ph.D.

TRAVEL

- "Fun on the Run" by Cynthia L. Copeland
- "Trouble–Free Travel with Children" by Vicki Lansky

WOMAN'S HEALTH

- "Mother-Daughter Wisdom: Creating a Legacy of Physical and Emotional Health" by Dr. Christiane Northrup
- "Our Bodies, Ourselves: A New Edition for a New Era" by Boston Woman's Health Book Collective

PARENTING MAGAZINES

- FamilyFun
- Mom and Baby
- Nick Jr. Family
- Parenting
- Parents
- Brain, Child Magazine for thinking mothers

More Ideas

_____

_____

_____

_____

_____

1 2 . DEVELOPMENT

Milestones to Remember

The developmental process begins from the moment of conception and spans through the adolescent years. Children pass through many facets of developmental growth, including gross and fine motor, language, social, emotional, and self-help skills. It is most rapid and memorable in the early years, where milestones are encouraged and marked with excitement, praise, and photos!

Development is a continuous process that occurs in an orderly sequence. Although development varies greatly amongst children, there is still a natural curiosity as to how our children are progressing when compared to others. The following section will help you chart your child's unique growth patterns. Should you have any concerns regarding your child's development, don't hesitate to discuss them with your pediatrician, or directly with an early intervention specialist.

A Note on Reflexes

Innate primary reactions are primitive reflexes found in newborns. Each reflex lasts for a few months, and then becomes integrated into the voluntary movement of the baby. If the reflex lasts for longer than the specified period, it may be something you should mention to your pediatrician.

1. **Moro (startle) Reflex:** a loud noise near the infant's head or a sudden "dropping" of the baby backward will cause the infant to throw their arms out to the side and then bring them in to their chest. Lasts from birth to 6 months.

2. **Grasp Reflex:** applying pressure in the palm of the hand causes baby to grasp the object tightly and resist removal of it. Lasts from birth to 3 or 4 months.

3. **Rooting Reflex:** stroking the outward corner of the baby's mouth causes the baby's lower lip, tongue, and head to move toward the stimulus. Lasts from birth to 3 or 4 months.

4. **Sucking Reflex:** placing a finger or nipple on the baby's lips causes the baby to begin sucking. Lasts from birth to 3 or 4 months.

The First Year – A Month at a Time

DATE & COMMENTS

Gross Motor
- Has strong reflex movements; moves arms, legs and hands energetically
- Can move body by digging heels into mattress then thrusting with legs
- Briefly lifts head up to 45 degrees when on tummy
- Moves head from side to side

Fine Motor
- Blinks at bright lights
- Looks at colorful object for a few seconds
- Focuses 8 to 18 inches away
- When lying on back, eyes will follow a moving person
- Will grasp and grip something if placed in their hand, then quickly drops it

Cognitive
- Will stop moving and move eyes toward a source of sound
- Distinguishes volume and pitch of sounds, prefers high-toned voices
- Alert for about 1 in 10 hours
- Stops sucking to look at something

Language
- Makes animal-like sounds such as grunts, groans and gurgles
- Cries when hungry or uncomfortable
- Has vague and impassive expression when awake

Social/Emotional
- Shows both excitement and distress
- Prefers to look at patterns or faces
- Makes brief, 1-2 second eye contact
- Smiles reflexively
- Enjoys and needs a great deal of physical contact

Self-Help
- Sleeps between 19 and 20 hours per day
- Feeds 7 to 8 times per day
- Roots for breast, even if not nursing
- May or may not enjoy sponge baths

SECOND MONTH

Gross Motor
- Muscle tone begins to improve; moves arms and legs smoothly
- Kicks legs like a bicycle
- Holds head fairly erect when in sitting position, although still wobbles
- Can roll on to back when placed on side

Fine Motor
- Stares vaguely at surroundings
- Visually follows object from left or right to center of body
- Reaches for and bats at objects

Cognitive
- Stays awake for longer periods, about an hour at a time
- Gets excited at a person's presence and watches alertly and directly
- Interested in sounds
- Picks out mother's voice from a group of voices

Language
- Makes sucking sounds
- Coos, grunts, and sighs

Social/Emotional
- Prefers to watch people over objects
- May imitate your smile
- Responds differently to voices, people, and tastes
- Continues to quiet when picked up and sees parent

Self-Help
- Has a smooth suck-swallow-breath pattern when feeding
- Sleeps nights for 4 to 10 hours at a time
- Beginning to organize a day/night schedule
- Feeds less often, with a more predictable feeding schedule

THIRD MONTH

Gross Motor

- Brings own body up compactly when picked up
- Leans on elbows when on tummy
- Holds head and chest up for a few seconds when lying on tummy
- Has more stable head and body control; bears weight on legs when held

Fine Motor

- Coordinates eye movements in a circle when watching a light or an object
- Eyes and head follow an object 180 degrees
- Reaches toward a toy without grasping it
- If offered a toy, will grasp and shake it

Cognitive

- Recognizes breast or bottle and squirms in anticipation
- Explores own face, eyes, and mouth with hand
- Studies movement of their own hands
- Begins to play with a rattle

Language

- Cries vary in pitch, length, and volume to make needs known
- Increases facial expressions and vocalizations
- Distinguishes speech from other sounds
- Laughs, chuckles, gurgles and coos in response to sounds

Social/Emotional

- Smiles easily and spontaneously, as well as voluntarily
- Crying decreases
- Begins to recognize familiar people

Self-Help

- Night wakening decreases in frequency and duration; may sleep through the night
- Gums objects and drools
- Benefits from predictable routines and predictable patterns, such as eating, sleeping and playing

FOURTH MONTH

Gross Motor

- Sits with assistance and support
- Rolls over from tummy to back
- Holds head steady and erect for short periods
- Turns head in all directions

Fine Motor

- Bats at objects with closed fists
- Reaches for a toy and grasps it momentarily
- Grasps a dangling toy and brings it toward mouth

Cognitive

- Interested in smells
- May prefer a particular toy
- Enjoys repeating a newly learned activity
- Uses hand and mouth for sensory exploration of objects

Language

- Smiles and vocalizes more toward an actual face, vs. a picture
- Laughs when playing
- Squeals

Social/Emotional

- Tries to attract attention to self when parent or sibling is nearby
- Plays with own hands, feet, fingers, toes
- Interested in/may smile at mirror image
- Stops unexplained crying
- Vocalizes in response to adult talk and smiles

Self-Help

- Watches others eat and shows interest in their food
- May be ready to start solid foods; swallows strained or pureed foods
- Recognizes bottle or breast visually
- Kicks and splashes in bath

FIFTH MONTH

Gross Motor

- Moves by rocking, twisting or rolling
- Rolls partway to side when lying on back
- Brings feet to mouth and may suck on toes
- Lifts both arms and feet when lying on tummy

Fine Motor

- Plays with a rattle when placed in hand
- Reaches and grasps a toy more solidly and begins to reach with both hands
- Holds bottle with both hands
- Wants to touch, hold, turn, shake, and mouth objects

Cognitive

- Finds partially hidden object
- Distinguishes between smells
- Turns head and neck to locate sounds
- Interested in simple board books

Language

- Interested in making new sounds such as squeals, grunts and makes a "raspberry" sound
- Cries when play is disrupted
- Experiments with mouth and sounds

Social/Emotional

- Smiles/vocalizes to attract attention and make social contact
- Imitates facial expressions
- Likes playing peek-a-boo, and pat-a-cake

Self-Help

- Sleeps 10-12 hours at night, with brief night awakening
- Naps 2-3 times per day for 1-4 hours
- Places both hands on bottle or breast
- May enjoy the introduction of, and has preferences for pureed foods with varied textures, tastes, and smells

SIXTH MONTH

Gross Motor

• When lying on back, may move by kicking against a solid surface	
• Rolls from back to tummy	
• Sits with little support; may lean forward onto hands for balance	
• Creeps – tries to move by propelling self on stomach with legs (often goes backwards)	
• Stands firmly when held	

Fine Motor

• Grasps a large ring	
• Begins to pass object from hand to hand	
• Holds small object in each hand	
• Bangs an object on the table	

Cognitive

• Alert at least half of waking hours	
• Likes looking at objects upside down	
• Distinguishes between friendly and angry voices	

Language

• Babbles to people	
• Vocalizes pleasure and displeasure	
• Coos, hums, squeals	

Social/Emotional

• Prefers a particular toy	
• Expresses different emotions (happiness, sadness), and may have abrupt mood changes (temperament)	
• May cry when parent leaves the room	
• May have an attachment to a significant object, such as a blanket or a stuffed animal	

Self-Help

• Holds, sucks, bites cookie or cracker and begins chewing	
• Likes to play with food	
• Uses tongue to move food around mouth	
• Continues sleeping and napping pattern	

SEVENTH MONTH

Gross Motor
- Sits alone
- Stands with support
- Pushes up on hands and knees and rocks back and forth
- Balances head well in all situations

Fine Motor
- Rotates wrist to turn and manipulate objects
- Grasps objects with fingers instead of entire hand
- Rakes tiny objects

Cognitive
- Understands that objects don't disappear when hidden
- Looks for family members or pets when named
- Tries to acquire desired, out-of-reach object
- Developing "cause and effect" concept

Language
- Imitates sounds, and series of sounds
- Learns meaning of "no" by tone of voice
- Shouts for attention

Social/Emotional
- Plays energetically with noise-making toys
- Touches toy or adult hand to restart an activity
- Shows humor and teases by laughing
- Smiles at own image in mirror
- May display stranger anxiety

Self-Help
- Holds cup handle and sips from a cup
- Holds own bottle
- Holds spoon and puts in food
- Beginning hand to mouth with spoon
- Naps 2 times per day

Gross Motor

- Crawls backward
- Uses furniture to pull self to standing position
- Stands if leaning against an object
- Moves from lying to sitting without help

Fine Motor

- Claps and waves hands
- Holds and manipulates one object while watching another
- Bangs two objects together at middle of body

Cognitive

- Enjoys lap games and finger plays
- Looks for dropped objects
- Solves simple problems, such as pulling on an object to retrieve it
- Visually follows path of a quickly moving object

Language

- Vocalizes several sounds in one breath
- Mimics mouth and jaw movements of others
- Responds to own name specifically

Social/Emotional

- Attached to parents, and shows anxiety when separated
- Pushes away undesirable objects
- May be fearful in previously accepted situations
- Imitates familiar gestures
- Plays 2-3 minutes with a single toy

Self-Help

- May sleep 11 to 13 hours a night with two naps per day
- Feeds self finger foods
- Tastes most everything and shows definite preferences and dislikes
- May drink from sippy cup

NINTH MONTH

Gross Motor

- Makes a few stepping movements forward if holding onto adult hands
- Stands up if holding onto something
- May attempt to move along furniture while standing and holding on
- Crawls forward
- Climbs easily and crawls up stairs

Fine Motor

- Reaches for a large object with both hands
- Picks up and manipulates two objects, one in each hand
- Reaches for small objects with finger and thumb – the "pincer grip"
- Mostly uses one hand at a time and alternates hand and arm movements

Cognitive

- Understands simple instructions, such as "sit down," "come here" and "give it to me"
- Uncovers a toy they see hidden
- Protects self and possessions

Language

- Imitates sounds, such as coughs and hisses
- Says "dada" or "mama", but may not be in reference to dad or mom
- May gesture to communicate desires such as shaking head "no"

Social/Emotioal

- Imitates play behaviors
- Purposefully chooses toy for play
- Performs for audience and repeats if applauded
- Shows preferences for people, places, objects

Self-Help

- Drinks from cup held for them
- Drools less (except while teething)
- Bites food voluntarily
- Holds limbs stiff to assist with dressing and undressing

TENTH MONTH

Gross Motor

- Stands momentarily with little support
- May be able to rise to a standing position independently
- Responds to music by rocking, bouncing, swaying, and humming
- May bend down to reach an object while holding onto something for support

Fine Motor

- Carries two small objects in one hand
- Interested in fitting things together
- Takes things out of containers
- Pokes with index finger

Cognitive

- Increasingly imitates others' actions
- Understands and obeys some words and commands
- Searches for toy if sees it hidden
- Listens selectively to familiar words
- Imitates action of toy manually, such as pushing toy car on floor

Language

- Repeats a word or nonsense syllable incessantly and uses it to answer every question
- Turns head when own name is heard
- Points with finger

Social/Emotional

- Likes playing in water
- Shows moods: hurt, happy, sad, angry
- Imitates facial expressions, sounds, and gestures

Self-Help

- Sleeps 12 to 14 hours at night
- Naps once or twice each day
- Uses coordinated movements to chew food
- Mimics scooping motion of food with spoon, and tries to bring it to mouth

ELEVENTH MONTH

Gross Motor
- Climbs up and down from small chairs
- Walks holding onto furniture
- Walks holding onto adult with both hands
- May take a step without holding onto anything

Fine Motor
- Takes lids off boxes
- Turns pages of book
- Nests objects, such as boxes or cups
- May grasp a crayon

Cognitive
- Recognizes words as symbols for objects; knows sheep "baas"
- Opens kitchen drawers and cabinets
- Removes rings from a stack
- Knows what "no-no" means and reacts
- Responds to simple verbal requests

Language
- Imitates speech rhythms and inflections
- Speaks a few intelligible words
- Shows understanding of words with appropriate behaviors or gestures
- Babbles with inflection imitating an adult
- Understands names of familiar objects and people

Social/Emotional
- Begins to learn sexual identity
- Asserts self among siblings
- Seeks approval and tries to avoid disapproval
- Engages in parallel play with another child
- Tests parental reactions at feedings and bedtime

Self-Help
- Finger feeds self entire meals
- Holds cup and drinks from it
- May untie shoes or pat Velcro in place
- Pulls off socks and shoes

Gross Motor

- Walks with one hand held, and may walk without help
- Creeps up and down stairs
- May get to standing position by pushing up from squatting
- Able to kneel

Fine Motor

- May show preference for use of one hand over another for a time, then switches again
- Twists covers off of containers
- May attempt to imitate a scribble with crayon and paper

Cognitive

- Learning correct use of toys such as using a telephone or putting a pot on toy stove
- Identifies animals in pictures
- Responds to directions, such as "pick up the toy" and "stop"
- Searches for hidden objects if they haven't seen it, but remembers where they last saw it

Language

- May speak 2 or 3 words
- Says "mama" or "dada" to name parent
- Repeats sounds and gestures if laughed at
- Babbles to self when alone
- Waves bye-bye

Social/Emotional

- Gives affection to people and favored objects
- Explores environment enthusiastically
- "Dances" to music
- Enjoys looking at pictures in books

Self-Help

- May resist new foods and being fed; insists on feeding self
- May resist napping
- Cares for doll or a soft toy by hugging, feeding and cuddling
- May mimic washing face
- Holds a toothbrush, although usually just chews on it

Gross Motor

- Develops full walking ability and may begin running
- Initially throws a ball underhanded, mostly in sitting position and improves to overhand while standing
- Crawls up and down stairs, then walks up one step at a time
- Seat themselves in small chair
- May climb out of crib or playpen

Fine Motor

- Stacks objects – builds a 2 cube tower
- Fills containers with objects then dumps them out
- Points at objects in the distance
- Scribbles on paper with a crayon
- Begins to show a hand preference

Cognitive

- May know some body parts
- Able to pick an object out of a familiar grouping such as a ball, bottle, and doll, when asked "get me the ball"
- Turns pages in a book, attends to pictures and will point to named objects
- Imitates household activities, such as cleaning and talking on the phone

NOTE ON LANGUAGE DEVELOPMENT: Until age 3, the average number of words a child will put together (not imitating) equals the child's age. For example, a 1 year old speaks single words, a 2 year old speaks 2-word sentences, etc.

Language

- Vocabulary: 12-15 months: 10-15 words
  15-18 months: 25-50 words
- Can identify one or two familiar objects, such as a book, doll, and blanket
- Babbles in a singing voice to music
- Asks for more food and names desired foods
- Babbling occurs at this age with some understandable words and some not
- Acts out needs if unable to say the words

Social/Emotional

- May show stranger anxiety
- Affectionate with hugs and kisses
- Seeks independence
- Temper tantrums may begin
- "No" is a heavily used word

Self-Help

- Stops drinking from a bottle
- Brings spoon to mouth with some spilling
- Transitions from two naps to one, possibly in the afternoon
- Brushes teeth with help
- Dressing: able to pull off hat, socks, or mittens, and assists with diaper changes and dressing by moving arms and legs appropriately

Gross Motor
- Pushes and pulls large toys
- Kicks a ball forward
- Rides on toys without pedals
- Walks down stairs with one hand held

Fine Motor
- Builds a 4-6 cube tower
- Turns one page at a time in a board book
- Makes circular scribbles and paints on paper provided
- Threads large-holed beads with stiff cording
- Holds a crayon with thumb and fingers instead of fist
- Imitates drawing a vertical line

Cognitive
- Matches sounds to animals
- Engages in nursery rhymes, finger plays, silly songs and repetitive books
- Begins to sort objects and categories, such as one group of horses and one group of dolls
- Recognizes self in a photograph
- Identifies at least three body parts

Language
- Babbling replaced by 30-70 words
- Begins to use own name when referring to self
- Imitates familiar animal sounds
- Tries to sing songs with words
- Names 2-5 pictures in books
- Imitates and uses two word phrases

Social/Emotional
- May show signs of jealousy
- Feels that the world revolves around them, and wants to be in control
- May become easily frustrated
- Plays alone for short time periods
- Possessive of toys

Self-Help
- Feeds self and gives back empty meal plate
- Stops mouthing inedible objects
- Loves to "help" around the house
- Naps once a day
- Dressing: undresses completely except for buttons and snaps, attempts to put on shoes, and unzips and zips a large zipper with assistance

Gross Motor

- Catches a large ball
- Rides a tricycle
- Walks up and down stairs alone … one step at a time
- Jumps in place
- May initiate climbing

Fine Motor

- Builds 6-8 cube towers
- Holds scissors and may attempt snipping
- Duplicates a circle
- Folds paper
- Developing a proper thumb and two finger grasp of crayon

Cognitive

- Follows routines
- Will show you their favorite characters or objects in books
- Begins dramatic play
- Matches circles, triangles, squares, and simple pictures
- Enjoys story times at the library
- Identifies purpose of simple objects like a telephone and broom

Language

- Parents understand most of what child says
- Imitates up to 4 word phrases
- Sings along to common songs
- Can say three word sentences
- Names five pictures on flashcards
- Eager to learn new words and may become frustrated when misunderstood
- Answers simple questions
- Speaks in two word sentences on average
- Points to eight body parts

24-30 MONTHS

Social/Emotional

- May have difficulty playing "with" other children; however, exposure to others is important
- Identifies self by name
- Tends to dawdle
- "MINE" will be a word you will hear often
- Needs to be warned about dangers, such as running into the street
- Fears emerge

Self-Help

- Brushes teeth with minimal help
- Begins to use a fork
- Problems with constipation may begin
- Definite likes and dislikes of food, and may become more "picky"
- May resist napping, but needs "quiet" time
- Dressing: puts on simple clothes without assistance, such as a hat and pants

30-36 MONTHS

Gross Motor

- Walks up stairs using alternating feet
- Hops on one foot
- Climbs well on climbing structures and ladders
- Runs very well

Fine Motor

- Builds a 9 cube tower
- Imitates drawing a horizontal line
- Snips on a line with scissors
- Copies circle already drawn
- Strings 1/2 inch beads

Cognitive

- Completes 3 - 4 piece puzzles
- Understands sizes, small or large and stacks rings in correct order
- Can count to 10
- Loves books, being read to, and "reading" alone
- Plays house
- Knows most body parts

Language

- Familiar adults understand most of what is said
- Tells you their needs, such as "I'm hungry" and "I want to play"
- Tells you stories and experiences they've had
- Tells you their name, age, and town they live in
- Asks tons of questions using what, where, and when
- Gets frustrated when not understood
- Names many pictures on flash cards

Social/Emotional

- Wants to do things independently with success and loves praise
- Starts to obey and follow rules, and understands consequences
- May have a hard time transitioning from one activity to the next
- Likes to create, but often needs help to complete the task
- Loves group circle time and interactive games with others
- Expresses concern for others

Self-Help

- Wants to help with adult tasks, such as setting and clearing the table
- Starts to remember dreams, and may have bad ones
- Naps may have stopped
- Likes pouring liquids such as "tea" at a tea party
- Dressing: puts on coat, dress and shirt (except for buttoning), able to undo large buttons, snaps, and shoelaces

Gross Motor

- Throws balls overhand and catches with arms extended
- Walks up and down stairs with alternating feet
- Carries a tray
- Climbs ladders on playground equipment

Fine Motor

- Copies a circle
- Cuts paper in half
- Rolls a "snake" and makes balls out of play dough
- Winds up toy

Cognitive

- Listens to stories and recalls portions of them
- Identifies some colors
- Sings songs from memory
- Counts objects
- Thinks of activities they want to do

Language

- Uses plural "s," "ing," possessive "s," and past-tense "ed," although often uses incorrectly
- Speaks well enough that a stranger can understand
- Speaks 3 – 5 word sentences
- May begin to imitate and mimic words you say...be careful!
- "Why?" is a favorite word now

Social/Emotional

- Begins to cooperate with other children and shares toys and takes turns
- Uses words to express emotions
- Becomes more independent in all areas
- Requires praise and encouragement when learning something new

Self-Help

- Turns faucet on and off and washes and dries hands
- Turns door knob and opens door
- Serve themselves food, such as pouring cereal, spreading jam on toast
- Brushes teeth and combs hair
- Selects own clothing, but may need help with weather appropriateness
- Loves to help mix baking ingredients
- Dressing: undresses fully, still needs help with buttons and orienting to front, back, and inside out, and left and right shoes

Gross Motor

- Jumps over objects, gallops and somersaults
- Bounces and catches a ball
- Hangs from monkey bar

Cognitive

- Names 6-8 colors and 3-4 shapes
- Understands concepts of size and position (the doll is on the bed)
- Tells made up stories
- Asks "how?" and "why?"
- Follows simple rules
- Counts objects up to 10
- Begins to rhyme

Fine Motor

- Traces letters and numbers
- May print name
- Holds writing utensil properly, using thumb and index/middle fingers (tripod grasp)
- Draws recognizable pictures
- Copies geometric shapes (circles, squares, cross)

Language

- Pretends to read books or newspapers
- Language is used well now and they can express their needs nicely
- Speaks 6-8 word sentences
- Links one and two sentences together
- Recognizes some letters
- Will share all ideas that come to mind

Social/Emotional

- Has a very active imagination and participates in make believe play with a storyline
- Says "please" and "thank you"
- Willing to try new things
- Questions differences in gender and race to define who they are

Self-Help

- Puts garbage into a trash pail
- Washes and dries face and brushes teeth independently
- May bathe independently with help to wash hair
- Helps with some meal preparation
- Dressing: dresses and undresses with little assistance, puts shoes on correct feet, needs help with tying, but can do Velcro and buckles

Gross Motor
- Marches rhythmically to music and skips
- Increased poise and coordination
- Walks up and kicks a ball

Fine Motor
- Hand preference is fully established
- Makes recognizable figures out of play dough
- Copies a triangle
- Ties knots

Cognitive
- Will remember the plans for the day and will sequence the activities accordingly
- Learning captures their attention making it a perfect time to attend concerts, productions, and museums
- Separates fact from fantasy
- Completes 25 piece puzzle

Language
- Has a large and continuously expanding vocabulary (approximately 2000 words)
- Answers telephone and finds person requested
- Delivers two part verbal messages

Social/Emotional
- Has a basic sense of right from wrong
- Cooperates and takes turns
- Understands when they are being punished or praised and will respond accordingly
- Chooses their own friends
- Plays competitive board and card games

Self-Help
- Prepares sandwich
- Can help fold and sort laundry and match socks
- Wipes nose with tissue
- Toilets independently and may or may not stay dry at night
- Can make own bed
- Dressing: dresses and undresses without assistance, buttons small buttons, and learns to tie shoelaces

13. WEBSITE RESOURCES

BABIES

www.aap.org
The American Academy of Pediatrics site offering a plethora of information regarding your child's health.

www.babyzone.com
Comprehensive website supplying a wide variety of information for parents.

www.drgreene.org
Doctor sponsored site dedicated to the health of babies and children.

www.great-beginnings.com
Links for helping and support for breastfeeding.

www.keepkidshealthy.com
Pediatricians guide to your children's health and safety.

www.lamaze.org
Child birth education.

www.motherwear.com
Online store offering breastfeeding supplies and clothing.

www.promom.org
Promotion of Mother's Milk, Inc., increasing public awareness and acceptance of breastfeeding.

www.colichelp.com
Offers support and information about your crying baby.

OUTWARD BOUND

www.bugaboodaytrips.com
Stroller day trips for major cities in North America.

www.lilaguide.com
Pocket sized guides to major cities in North America.

www.madallie.com
Kids travel accessories.

HOT TOPICS

www.kidsgrowth.com
Great articles on everything to do with raising children, also has developmental profiles.

www.kidshealth.org
Providing doctor approved health information for children from birth to adolescence.

MEALS

www.foodallergy.org
Food allergy network.

www.foodsafety.gov
U.S. government information on food safety.

www.kidswithfoodallergies.org
Providing information, support and resources for families of children with food allergies.

www.wholesomebabyfood.com
Healthy recipes for baby, toddler, children.

www.savingdinner.com
Sign up for a weekly mailer providing nutritious meal ideas with grocery lists, nutritional outline, and more.

FAMILY

www.family.org
Website for "Focus on the Family" by psychologist James Dobson, renowned parenting, child and family expert.

www.familycorner.com
Devoted to family activities from crafts to recipes.

www.parentsplace.com
ivillage site offering a wide variety of resources for the whole family.

www.shutterfly.com
Wide variety of personalized photo gifts available, including: mugs, mouse pads, note cards, tote bags, aprons, frames, and canvas prints.

JUST FOR MOMS

www.DONA.org
Doula organization.

www.doulaworld.com
Information re: Doulas.

www.midwiferytoday.com
Wide-ranging site offering information about midwives and resources.

www.parentinghumor.com
Lighthearted and funny site dedicated to parenting.

www.manicmommies.com
Tips and ideas from the perspective of working moms. Great podcast.

HOUSEHOLD MANAGEMENT

www.cheapskatemonthly.com
Information for debt-free living.

www.flylady.net
Humorous site offering tips on organization and ideas for the busy mother.

FUN TIME

www.constplay.com
Constructive Playthings brand toys.

www.early-advantage.com
Educational resources, specifically for foreign language instruction.

www.guidecraft.com
Cutting edge educational toys.

www.iqkids.com
Award winning toys and games.

www.kidslearningdepot.com
Excellent toy site.

www.magiccabin.com
Assortment of toy offerings to spark the imagination.

www.mflp.com
"Music for Little People" catalog for music and materials.

www.novanatural.com
Natural wood and educational toys and books.

www.playstoretoys.com
Quality wooden and natural toys for creative and imaginative play.

www.preschooleducation.com
Many ideas for activities, games, educational information.

www.storybooktoys.com
Homemade wood toys and inspiring costumes.

www.educationaltoysplanet. com
Super toy site.

www.nienhuis.com
Toys for Life – Montessori-based learning materials.

SAFETY

www.cpsc.gov
U.S. Consumer Product Safety Commission – provides information about toy and child product recalls and water safety. Commission hotline: 1-800-638-2772.

www.kidsource.com
Extensive recall information posting board as well as in-depth articles on a variety of subjects including health and safety.

www.liliguanausa.org
Kid friendly safety products designed to help kids to recognize possible dangerous situations and what to do.

www.noburns.com
Offers great tips to prevent scalding of children and site to order the heat sensing Rubber Ducky.

www.safekids.org
National SAFE KIDS campaign – unintentional injury prevention.

www.recalls.gov
Comprehensive recall site.

DEVELOPMENT

www.cdc.gov/actearly
National Center on Birth Defects and Developmental Disabilities. Comprehensive site offering milestones and warning signs in development.

www.firstsigns.org
Resources regarding early detection and intervention of developmental disorders and delays.

Note: These websites were current at the time of publication.

Bibliography

Breastfeeding Information Guide:
Medela, Inc. Illinois: McHenry, 2000.

Curtis, Glade B., M.D. and Schuler, Judith, M.S.
Your Baby's First Year Week by Week.
Tucson: Fisher Books, 2000.

Eiseberg, Arlene, Murkoff, Heidi E.,
and Hathaway, Sandee E., B.S.N.
What to Expect the Toddler Years.
New York: Workman Publishing, 1994.

Hawaii Early Learning Profile.
Vort, Corp, 1994.

Pagel, Danita, and Thomas, E. John.
The Ultimate Book of Kid Concoctions.
Ohio: The Kid Concoctions Company, 1998.

Pratt, Pat Nuse, and Allen, Anne Stevens.
Occupational Therapy for Children.
2nd edition. St. Louis:
The C.V. Mosby Company, 1989.

Rogers, Sally J., et al.
Early Intervention Developmental Profile.
2nd edition. Ann Arbor:
University of Michigan Press, 1981.

Sears, William, M.D., and Sears, Martha, R.N.
The Family Nutrition Book.
Boston: Little, Brown and Company, 1999.

Shelov, Steven P., M.D.
*Caring for Your Baby and
Young Child Birth to Age 5*.
New York: Bantam Books, 1994.

*The Good Housekeeping Illustrated
Book of Pregnancy and Baby Care*.
New York: Hearst Books, 1999.

Telep, Valya. (1997).
Tips on Toys.
Retrieved June 21, 2005, from Virginia State
University, a Virginia Cooperative Extension
**www.ext.vt.edu/pubs/family/350-063/
350-063.html**

Jones, Michelle. (n.d).
Homemade Art Supply List.
Retrieved June 21, 2005, from
**www.blessingsforlife.com/crafts/home
made_art_supplies.html**

*The New Parents Guide: Toddler Products
for the Third Year*. (2005).
Retrieved March 31, 2005, from
**www.thenewparentsguide.com/essential-
baby-products-basics-thirdyear.html**

Hints for Working Moms
(n.d.). Retrieved May 1, 2005, from
**www.verybestbaby.com/content/article.
asp?section=fm&id=20011041651361
680157**

All About Moms: Diaper Bag Checklist.
(n.d.). Retrieved February 23, 2005, from
**www.allaboutmoms.com/allaboutmoms/
diaperbagchecklist.html**

All About Moms: Babysitter Checklist.
(n.d.). Retrieved February 23, 2005, from
www.allaboutmoms.com/guide.htm

Born to Read. (2005)
Retrieved December 12, 2005,
from American Library Association
www.ala.org/alsc/raiseareader.html

Constipation Treatment Guide. (2003)
Retrieved February 25, 2005, from
**www.keepkidshealthy.com/welcome/
treatmentguides/constipation.html**

Forbidden foods for baby.
(n.d.) Retrieved May 1, 2005, from
**www.verybestbaby.com/content/article.
asp?section=fb&id=20011011212341575774**

American Library Association.
"Born to Read: How to Raise a Reader".
Association for Library Service to
Children. 2003. Retrieved May 3, 2006.
**www.ala.org/ALSCTemplate.cfm?Section=
borntoread&Template=/ContentManage
ment/HTMLDisplay.cfm&ContentID=9945**

Contributors

We would like to thank the following friends and family for their thoughtful contributions to this book. Without their wonderful tips, ideas and editing this book would not have been possible. We are proud to be on this parenthood journey with you!

Teresa Axten
Noelle Balsamo
Karin Beauregard
Kelly Beins
Michelle McNamara
Jeanette Berube
Beth Birmingham
April Bolden
Christine Braga
Monique Bryant
Christine Burgess
Carol Callan
Rebecca Caruso
Lisa Clifton
Marli Cline
Holly Cole
Ann Conte
Renee Cooney
Shannon Dickson
Tammy Doering

Grace Emma
Elizabeth Ferris
Kathleen Ferris
Ida Gopan
Jane Gopan
Jody Fitzgerald Haseltine
Shannon Hays
Karolyn Heubner
Katharine Heubner
Alyssa Hoard
Charlotte Jerace
Allison King
Shari Kleinman
Amy Kostka
Renate Kostka
Lisa Lunsford
Sheila McAdams
Andrea McKee
Kimberly Moreau
Colleen Parsons
Dee Partridge

Jill Peterson
Marjorie Pratt
Kimberly Putney
Sarah Rose
Nicole Saadvandi
Sara Scotch
Patti Stark
Nicole Surrett
Juliette Tardiff
Dr. Carolyn Thumser
Barbara Tocci
Diane Tocci
Lila Tocci
Ruth Tocci
Qi Tu
Christine Townsley
Christine Van Bloem
Heather Wheat
Trish Williams
Jane Wolbach

Thank You

First and foremost, thank you to our amazing husbands, Scott and VJ for their patience and support. On many evenings after giving baths and reading bedtime stories we would vanish to labor on our "other baby" – we love you!

To Dr. Carolyn Thumser, our beloved and entrusted Pediatrician, who read and edited the manuscript to ensure we were medically accurate and "in tune" with what mothers are truly concerned about.

To Cynthia Tocci, for being a wonderful help to us whenever we called upon you. We are grateful to be a part of your Laurel Canyon Publishing family.

To Charlotte Jerace, for your encouragement, professional guidance and assistance throughout this project.

To our fantastic editors: Kimberly Putney, April Bolden, Lisa Lunsford and Allison King for tackling the many evolutions of this book. And Laurence Tocci, our "on-call" English expert.

To Elizabeth Ferris, for your computer brilliance and editing.

To Joanne Andrews, for our beautiful cover art.

To Lynn Wood, for designing a magnificent book – thanks for taking us on!

To Kelly Beins and Sheila McAdams, who went above and beyond the call of duty filling out the survey.

To John Chadis, and Grace Emma for your advice and help with the publishing world.